Horizons
Mathematics 2

Book 2

by
Sareta A. Cummins

Edited by
David J. Korecki

Illustrated by
Tye A. Rausch

Editorial Staff
Christine A. Korecki
John P. Robinett

Revisions
Alan Christopherson
Chris Burkholder
Annette Walker

Alpha Omega Publications, Inc.
Rock Rapids, IA

i

Horizons
Mathematics 2

Horizons Mathematics 2, Book 2 is only a *part* of a mathematics curriculum which consists of Horizons Mathematics 2, Book 1; Horizons Mathematics 2, Book 2; and Horizons Mathematics 2 Teacher's Guide. It is *necessary* to use the Teacher's Guide for a complete second grade mathematics program. The Teacher's Guide contains some essential concepts that are not presented in the student workbooks.

Media Credits:
Page 56: © Usagi-D, iStock, Thinkstock

Horizons Mathematics 2, Book 2
© MCMXCIII by Alpha Omega Publications, Inc.
804 N. 2nd Ave. E., Rock Rapids, IA 51246-1759

Printed in the United States of America
ISBN 978-1-58095-947-6

① Circle the least number.

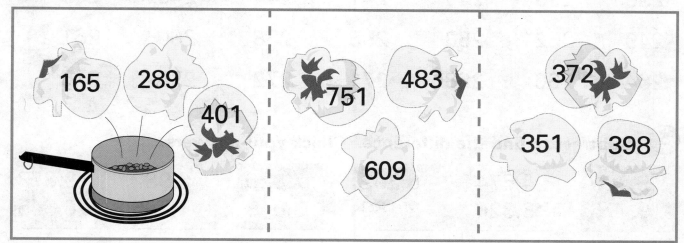

165 289 401 751 483 609 372 351 398

② Write as a number sentence.

Sixty-five and twenty-eight equals ninety-three. _____

Ten added to seventy-four equals eighty-four. _____

Forty-three plus seventeen equals sixty. _____

The sum of thirty-one and fifty-eight is eighty-nine. _____

Twenty-five increased by thirteen is thirty-eight. _____

③ Find the sum and check.

374	102	360	326	139	342	111
182	584	286	471	329	282	539
+211	+192	+312	+ 192	+220	+121	+133

450	431	332	122	212	471	172
173	215	130	228	236	253	443
+122	+191	+291	+ 349	+438	+151	+150

4 Put an X on the numbers out of sequence.

236	238	240	241	244	246	248
249	252	253	256	258	260	261
264	266	268	271	272	275	276

5 Subtract to find the difference. Check your answers.

9,780 - 9,175	4,574 - 3,326	6,392 - 2,183	7,826 - 3,018	6,982 - 1,765	9,873 - 6,545

8,931 - 4,225	6,941 - 3,512	8,931 - 2,407	7,690 - 5,439	8,497 - 3,019	4,651 - 2,529

6 Write the numbers.

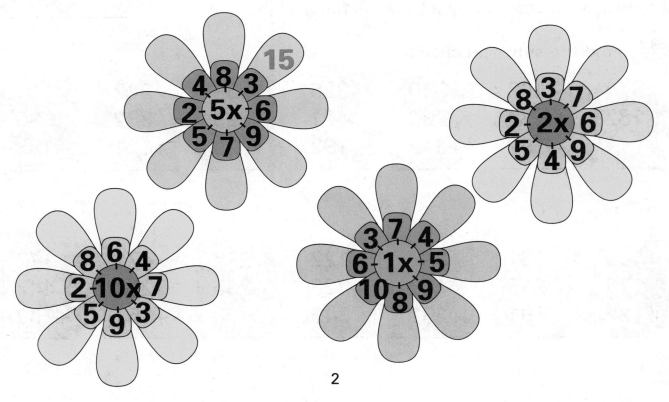

1 **Write the fraction that shows what part is shaded.**

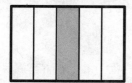 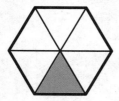 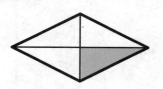 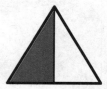

_____ _____ _____ _____

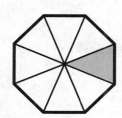 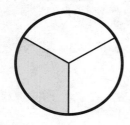 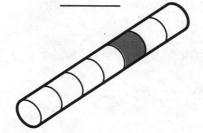 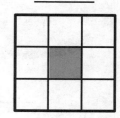

_____ _____ _____ _____

2 **Multiply to find the product.**

X	2	4	7	3	0	6	8	9	5	10	1
5											

X	7	1	4	6	3	9	0	10	8	2	5
2											

3 **Find the sum and check.**

171	184	417	228	216	241	185
259	355	296	277	395	386	296
+136	+316	+182	+ 270	+143	+109	+404
___	___	___	___	___	___	___

258	337		178	174
163	315		453	433
+112	+161		+101	+134
___	___		___	___

3

4 Write the value.

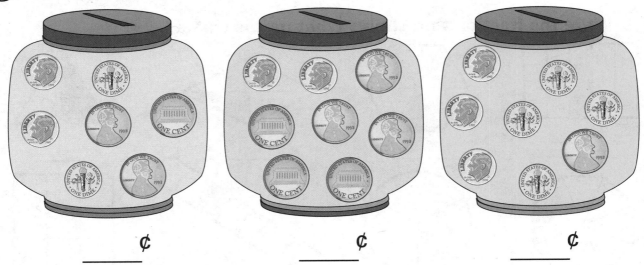

_____ ¢   _____ ¢   _____ ¢

5 Put an X on the numbers out of sequence.

603	606	609	614	615	618	620
624	627	631	633	635	639	642
645	646	651	654	657	662	663

6 Connect the dots counting by 2's.

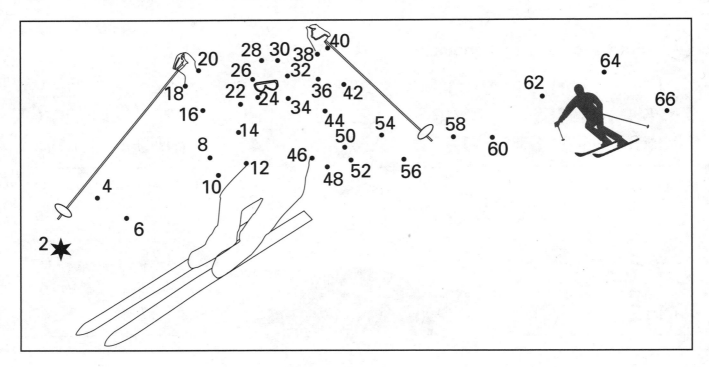

4

1 **Write the value.**

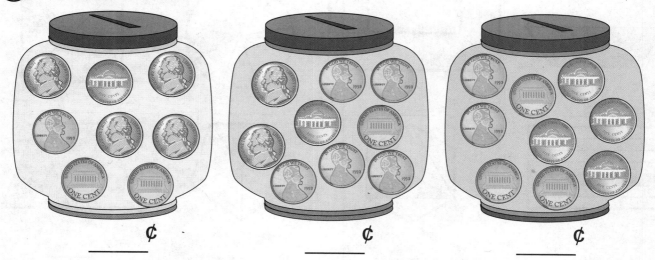

_____ ¢   _____ ¢   _____ ¢

2 **Write < or >.**

 _____   _____    _____

 _____   _____   _____

3 **Write 2 addition and 2 subtraction facts.**

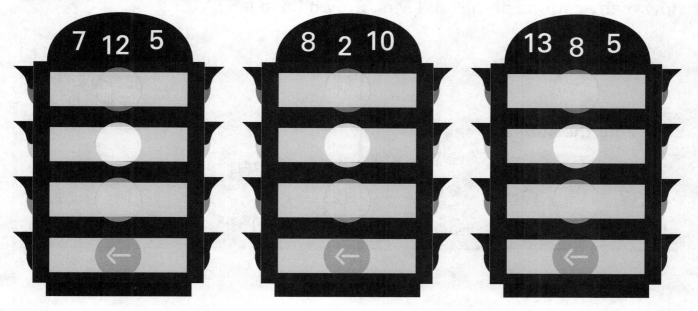

5

4 **Write the fraction that shows what part is shaded.**

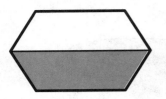 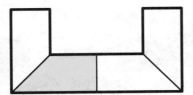 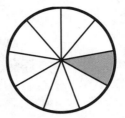 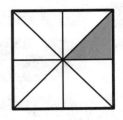

_____ _____ _____ _____

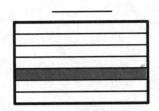 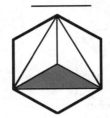  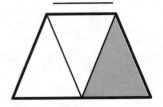

_____ _____ _____ _____

5 **Multiply to find the product.**

X	0	1	2
3			
5			
9			

X	2	5	10
1			
6			
8			

X	5	2	10
2			
4			
7			

6 Mrs. Brown has 126 cartons of milk to sell.
The second grade class took away 18 cartons for their lunch.
How many cartons of milk did Mrs. Brown have left?

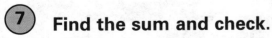

7 **Find the sum and check.**

242	354	128	262	261	385	420
137	227	251	165	117	163	139
+194	+243	+383	+ 453	+359	+424	+179

1 Write the number of coins needed.

38¢					
17¢					
46¢					
63¢					
84¢					

2 Write the answers.

Is 26 closer to 20 or 30? ___   Is 37 closer to 30 or 40? ___

Is 53 closer to 50 or 60? ___   Is 72 closer to 70 or 80? ___

3 Color the shape for each fractional part.

$\frac{1}{4}$ $\frac{1}{8}$ $\frac{1}{2}$ $\frac{1}{6}$

$\frac{1}{3}$ $\frac{1}{7}$ $\frac{1}{5}$ $\frac{1}{9}$

7

4 **Write as a number sentence.**

Fifty-seven take away thirty-three equals twenty-four. _____

Forty-eight decreased by eleven is thirty-seven. _____

Sixty-four minus eighteen equals forty-six. _____

Seventy-five less twenty is fifty-five. _____

5 **Write < or >.**

34¢ ____

58¢ ____

29¢ ____

72¢ ____

97¢ ____

6 **Find the sum and check.**

115	184	534	297	475	343	121
495	345	176	438	139	368	388
+276	+159	+182	+ 213	+261	+173	+228

7 Jan had $584 in her bank account. She took $275 out of it to buy a couch. How much did she have left in her banking account?

8

1 **Match the time equivalents.**

1 year	60 seconds	1 day	30 minutes
1 minute	7 days	1 hour	24 hours
1 year	365 days	1 year	52 weeks
1 week	12 months	$\frac{1}{2}$ hour	60 minutes

2 **Write < or >.**

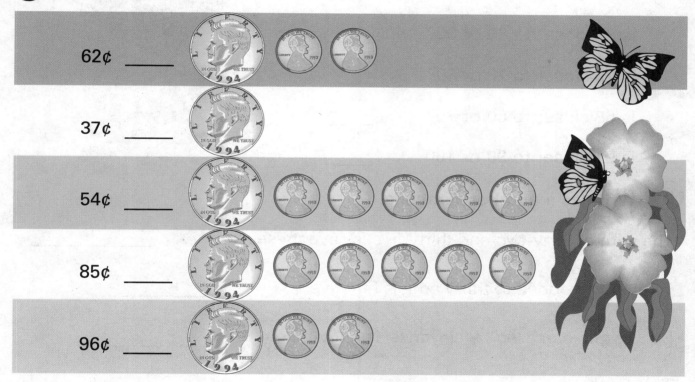

62¢ _____

37¢ _____

54¢ _____

85¢ _____

96¢ _____

3 **Shade the object for each fractional part.**

 $\frac{1}{6}$

 $\frac{1}{7}$

$\frac{1}{2}$ GO team!

 $\frac{1}{9}$

$\frac{1}{3}$ Goldilocks and the Three Bears

 $\frac{1}{5}$

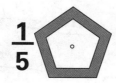 $\frac{1}{8}$ STOP

 $\frac{1}{4}$

9

④ Write the numbers.

9 + ___ = 14

___ + 4 = 5

4 + ___ = 8

6 + ___ = 11

2 + ___ = 6

___ + 3 = 11

___ + 1 = 9

___ + 9 = 9

___ + 8 = 14

3 + ___ = 8

9 + ___ = 12

___ + 6 = 8

___ + 8 = 13

5 + ___ = 10

7 + ___ = 15

⑤ Write the number.

Is 47 closer to 40 or 50?   _____

Is 82 closer to 80 or 90?   _____

Is 23 closer to 20 or 30?   _____

Is 68 closer to 60 or 70?   _____

Is 91 closer to 90 or 100?   _____

⑥ Write as a number sentence.

The sum of forty-two and thirty-five is seventy-seven.   _____

Twenty-five added to thirty equals fifty-five.   _____

Sixty-eight increased by eleven is seventy-nine.   _____

⑦ Write two addition and two subtraction facts.

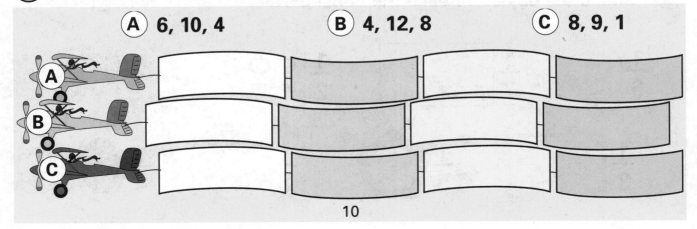

Ⓐ 6, 10, 4   Ⓑ 4, 12, 8   Ⓒ 8, 9, 1

1 **Write the numbers.**

four 3's = ___ + ___ + ___ + ___ = ___ x ___ = ___

eight 3's = ___ + ___ + ___ + ___ + ___ + ___ + ___ + ___ = ___ x ___ = ___

seven 3's = ___ + ___ + ___ + ___ + ___ + ___ + ___ = ___ x ___ = ___

six 3's = ___ + ___ + ___ + ___ + ___ + ___ = ___ x ___ = ___

three 3's = ___ + ___ + ___ = ___ x ___ = ___

nine 3's = ___ + ___ + ___ + ___ + ___ + ___ + ___ + ___ + ___ = ___ x ___ = ___

2 **Write the numbers.**

1 day = _____ hours	1 minute = _____ seconds
1 year = _____ days	1 year = _____ weeks
1 week = _____ days	1 year = _____ months
1 hour = _____ minutes	$\frac{1}{2}$ hour = _____ minutes

3 **Find the sum. Write even or odd.**

4 +8 _____	6 +2 _____	8 +6 _____	2 +8 _____
_____	_____	_____	_____

3 +5 _____	7 +9 _____	5 +7 _____	7 +3 _____
_____	_____	_____	_____

11

④ **Write the numbers.**

4 - ___ = 1	9 - ___ = 3	12 - ___ = 3
___ - 5 = 3	___ - 8 = 5	___ - 0 = 4
12 - ___ = 9	15 - ___ = 9	___ - 6 = 5
11 - ___ = 9	10 - ___ = 6	___ - 5 = 0
7 - ___ = 5	___ - 2 = 8	___ - 6 = 8

⑤ **Find the sum and check.**

3,242	2,449	2,320	1,017	2,438	1,130
1,581	2,165	3,295	3,296	1,042	2,589
+1,019	+2,243	+1,157	+3,522	+4,494	+ 4,055

⑥ **Write as a number sentence.**

Twenty-seven minus fifteen equals twelve.   _____

Forty-three decreased by twenty-eight is fifteen.   _____

Fifty-nine subtracted from sixty-six equals seven.   _____

Eighty-two take away thirty-four is forty-eight.   _____

⑦ **Multiply to find the product.**

X	5
3	
8	
5	
7	
9	

X	10
3	
8	
5	
7	
9	

X	2
3	
8	
5	
7	
9	

X	0
3	
8	
5	
7	
9	

 **$1.00 one dollar 100¢**

 **$5.00 five dollars 500¢**
$5.00 equals five one dollar bills

 **$10.00 ten dollars 1,000¢**
$10.00 equals ten one dollar bills

 **$20.00 twenty dollars 2,000¢**
$20.00 equals twenty one dollar bills

1 **Write the value.**

$ _____ . _____

$ _____ . _____

(2) Find the sum. Write even or odd.

7 _____ +6 _____ _____	5 _____ +8 _____ _____	4 _____ +9 _____ _____	12 _____ +15 _____ _____
25 _____ +22 _____ _____	17 _____ +11 _____ _____	35 _____ +32 _____ _____	26 _____ +12 _____ _____

(3) Match the number families.

3 + 3	5 x 3
eight 3's	nine 3's
3 + 3 + 3 + 3 + 3	30
9 x 3	8 x 3
10 x 3	two 3's

3 + 3 + 3 + 3	seven 3's
five threes	3 + 3 + 3
7 x 3	4 x 3
three 3's	6 x 3
3 + 3 + 3 + 3 + 3 + 3	5 x 3

(4) Write = or ≠.

1 day _____ 12 hours	1 year _____ 356 days
1 year _____ 52 weeks	1 hour _____ 60 minutes
1 minute _____ 30 seconds	1 week _____ 7 days
$\frac{1}{2}$ hour _____ 60 minutes	1 year _____ 12 months

(5) Ed and Barb invited 183 people to their wedding. There were 28 people that said they could not come. How many planned on attending the wedding?

14

1 **Write the numbers.**

6 thousands + 5 hundreds + 4 tens + 3 ones = ___+___+___+___ = ___

4 thousands + 7 hundreds + 2 tens + 8 ones = ___+___+___+___ = ___

5 thousands + 9 hundreds + 3 tens + 1 one = ___+___+___+___ = ___

8 thousands + 1 hundred + 5 tens + 6 ones = ___+___+___+___ = ___

3 thousands + 0 hundreds + 7 tens + 4 ones = ___+___+___+___ = ___

2 **Write the numbers.**

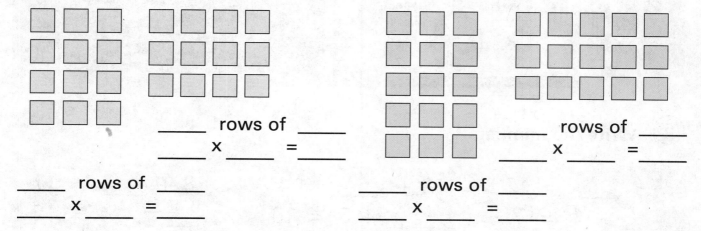

_____ rows of _____
_____ x _____ = _____

_____ rows of _____
_____ x _____ = _____

_____ rows of _____
_____ x _____ = _____

_____ rows of _____
_____ x _____ = _____

3 **Draw the hands on the clocks.**

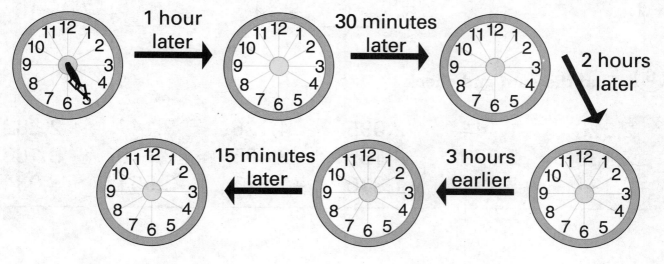

1 hour later   30 minutes later   2 hours later

15 minutes later   3 hours earlier

15

(4) **Write the value.**

$_____._____

$_____._____

(5) **Write the numbers.**

7 + ____ = 12	2 + ____ = 4	8 + ____ = 17
____ + 1 = 7	____ + 3 = 10	____ + 4 = 12
4 + ____ = 8	5 + ____ = 5	6 + ____ = 15
2 + ____ = 9	____ + 3 = 7	____ + 1 = 5
7 + ____ = 14	5 + ____ = 14	____ + 7 = 10

(6) **Find the sum and check.**

2,326	1,144	2,095	4,126	3,147	2,282
2,139	2,079	4,165	3,465	2,178	3,168
+2,191	+3,231	+1,316	+1,273	+3,551	+3,034
_____	_____	_____	_____	_____	_____

16

1 **Match the fraction to its shaded part.**

$\dfrac{1}{6}$

$\dfrac{1}{4}$

$\dfrac{1}{8}$

$\dfrac{1}{3}$

$\dfrac{1}{5}$

$\dfrac{1}{2}$

2 **Match the multiplication pairs.**

3 x 6 = 18	3 x 1 = 3	4 x 3 = 12	8 x 3 = 24
3 x 7 = 21	7 x 3 = 21	3 x 8 = 24	9 x 3 = 27
2 x 3 = 6	6 x 3 = 18	5 x 3 = 15	3 x 4 = 12
1 x 3 = 3	3 x 2 = 6	3 x 9 = 27	3 x 5 = 15

3 **Write the numbers.**

6 thousands + 2 hundreds + 0 tens + 7 ones = _____ + _____ + _____ + _____ = _____

5 thousands + 6 hundreds + 1 ten + 2 ones = _____ + _____ + _____ + _____ = _____

4 thousands + 9 hundreds + 8 tens + 7 ones = _____ + _____ + _____ + _____ = _____

8 thousands + 7 hundreds + 3 tens + 0 ones = _____ + _____ + _____ + _____ = _____

3 thousands + 5 hundreds + 6 tens + 7 ones = _____ + _____ + _____ + _____ = _____

1 thousand + 4 hundreds + 9 tens + 5 ones = _____ + _____ + _____ + _____ = _____

4 **Draw both hands on the clocks.**

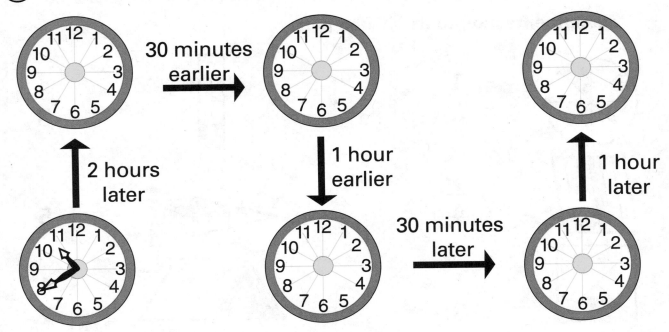

30 minutes earlier

2 hours later

1 hour earlier

30 minutes later

1 hour later

5 **Write the numbers.**

12 - ____ = 7	7 - ____ = 4	____ - 3 = 7
____ - 6 = 7	4 - ____ = 2	14 - ____ = 5
8 - ____ = 4	____ - 7 = 3	____ - 4 = 8
9 - ____ = 2	5 - ____ = 5	17 - ____ = 8
____ - 1 = 5	____ - 3 = 8	____ - 7 = 6

6 The basketball team scored 28 points in the first half and 34 points in the second half. They scored how many fewer points the first half than the second half?

There were 72 plums in one basket and 26 grapefruit in another. There were how many fewer grapefruit than plums?

① Write the value.   4 pts.

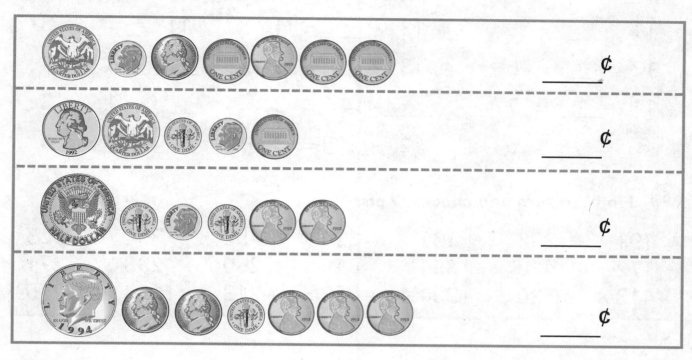

_____ ¢

_____ ¢

_____ ¢

_____ ¢

② Multiply to find the product.   18 pts.

0 x 0	1 x 1	1 x 2	10 x 6	0 x 8	10 x 4	3 x 1	10 x 3	2 x 0

5 x 0	6 x 1	4 x 0	10 x 7	5 x 1	10 x 9	0 x 6	10 x 8	1 x 7

③ Write as a number sentence.   4 pts.

The sum of thirty-five and fifty-three is eighty-eight.   _____

Twenty-seven increased by eleven equals thirty-eight.   _____

Forty added to sixty equals one hundred.   _____

Seventy-one plus fifteen equals eighty-six.   _____

19

4 Write the numbers. 15 pts.

____ - 4 = 6	____ - 8 = 6	____ - 3 = 3
11 - ____ = 5	13 - ____ = 4	11 - ____ = 3
12 - ____ = 6	13 - ____ = 6	____ - 6 = 4
11 - ____ = 7	____ - 4 = 3	____ - 1 = 3
8 - ____ = 6	12 - ____ = 9	____ - 3 = 6

5 Find the sum and check. 7 pts.

191	232	161	324	482	354	123
172	418	394	419	250	293	271
+413	+126	+334	+ 252	+213	+110	+275
____	____	____	____	____	____	____

6 Subtract to find the difference. Check your answers. 7 pts.

450	752	842	980	893	581	795
- 413	- 648	- 105	- 127	- 507	- 574	- 337
____	____	____	____	____	____	____

7 Karen sold 385 candy bars. Allen sold 257. Karen sold how many more candy bars than Allen?
How many candy bars did they sell in all?

Stephanie and Paul walked their dog, Missy, for 20 minutes on Monday, 15 minutes on Tuesday, and 35 minutes on Wednesday.
How many total minutes did they walk on Monday and Wednesday?

2 pts.

1 Multiply to find the product.

2 x 6	3 x 7	8 x 0	1 x 9	0 x 2	6 x 1	0 x 3	10 x 2	2 x 5
5 x 5	1 x 2	4 x 3	5 x 9	2 x 8	3 x 9	4 x 5	4 x 2	7 x 5
3 x 8	2 x 7	1 x 3	2 x 9	3 x 2	5 x 8	5 x 3	6 x 5	2 x 2

2 Draw both hands on the clocks for:

The time you get up in the morning

The time you get home from school

The time you eat lunch

The time you play

3 Write the numbers.

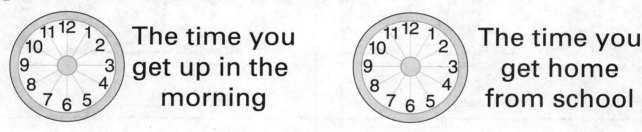

$1 + \underline{\quad} = 5$

$\underline{\quad} + 7 = 15$

$4 + \underline{\quad} = 6$

$\underline{\quad} + 0 = 7$

$9 + \underline{\quad} = 13$

$9 + \underline{\quad} = 17$

$3 + \underline{\quad} = 10$

$\underline{\quad} + 5 = 12$

$\underline{\quad} + 3 = 11$

$\underline{\quad} + 9 = 16$

$\underline{\quad} + 3 = 5$

$3 + \underline{\quad} = 4$

$1 + \underline{\quad} = 1$

$\underline{\quad} + 4 = 9$

$\underline{\quad} + 6 = 12$

4 Write = or ≠.

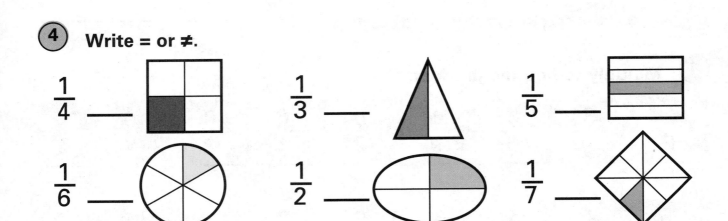

$\dfrac{1}{4}$ ___ $\dfrac{1}{3}$ ___ $\dfrac{1}{5}$ ___

$\dfrac{1}{6}$ ___ $\dfrac{1}{2}$ ___ $\dfrac{1}{7}$ ___

5 Write the value.

$ _____ . _____

$ _____ . _____

$ _____ . _____

$ _____ . _____

6 The auditorium at school will seat 380 people. The cafeteria will seat 175. How many fewer seats are there in the cafeteria than in the auditorium?

22

1 **Write the numbers.**

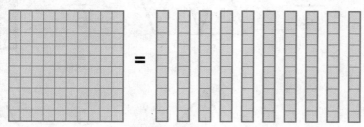

1 hundred   = 10 tens

3 hundreds = 2 hundreds + _____ tens

6 hundreds = 5 hundreds + _____ tens

8 hundreds = 7 hundreds + _____ tens

4 hundreds = 3 hundreds + _____ tens

7 hundreds = 6 hundreds + _____ tens

2 **Write the numbers.**

8 + _____ = 13	_____ + 6 = 12	7 - _____ = 4
_____ - 1 = 2	1 + _____ = 3	_____ + 3 = 10
_____ + 9 = 14	5 + _____ = 5	5 - _____ = 3
_____ - 0 = 1	_____ - 0 = 5	_____ + 5 = 10
10 - _____ = 5	9 + _____ = 16	13 - _____ = 9

3 **Multiply to find the product.**

X	3	1	7	0	4	9	6	2	8	5	10
2											

X	4	2	9	3	10	1	7	5	8	0	6
3											

23

4 Write = or ≠.

$\frac{1}{3}$ ___

$\frac{1}{4}$ ___

$\frac{1}{5}$ ___

$\frac{1}{8}$ ___

$\frac{1}{2}$ ___

$\frac{1}{6}$ ___

5 Find the sum and check:

197	248	202	194	132	119	336
183	275	388	279	145	482	180
+110	+243	+395	+ 423	+599	+283	+326

6 Subtract to find the difference.

973	894	762	893	341	954	382
- 869	- 346	- 248	- 504	- 128	- 318	- 215

694	240	785	963	470	882	576
- 585	- 119	- 479	- 239	- 246	- 863	- 437

7 Alice lives 283 miles from her grandmother. Anna lives 267 miles from her grandmother. Anna had how many fewer miles to travel to grandmother's than Alice?

I = 1   V = 5   X = 10   L = 50   C = 100   D = 500   M = 1,000

Roman numerals	I	II	III	IV	V	VI	VII	VIII	IX	X
Arabic numbers	1	2	3	4	5	6	7	8	9	10

① Write the Roman numerals.

11 = 10 + 1 = _____   16 = 10 + 6 = _____

12 = 10 + 2 = _____   17 = 10 + 7 = _____

13 = 10 + 3 = _____   18 = 10 + 8 = _____

14 = 10 + 4 = _____   19 = 10 + 9 = _____

15 = 10 + 5 = _____   20 = 10 + 10 = _____

② Write the value.

 $_____._____

  $_____._____

  $_____._____

25

③ Write the numbers.

4 hundreds   + 3 tens   = 3 hundreds   + _____ tens

7 hundreds   + 5 tens   = 6 hundreds   + _____ tens

2 hundreds   + 7 tens   = 1 hundred   + _____ tens

8 hundreds   + 2 tens   = 7 hundreds   + _____ tens

3 hundreds   + 6 tens   = 2 hundreds   + _____ tens

④ Multiply to find the product.

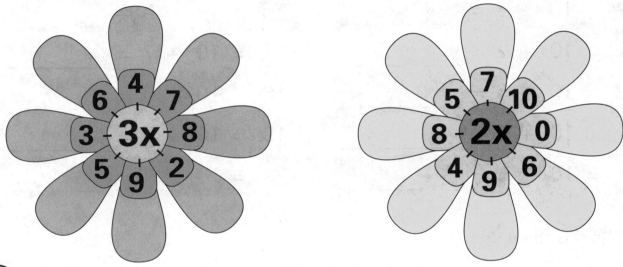

⑤ Circle the next shape in sequence.

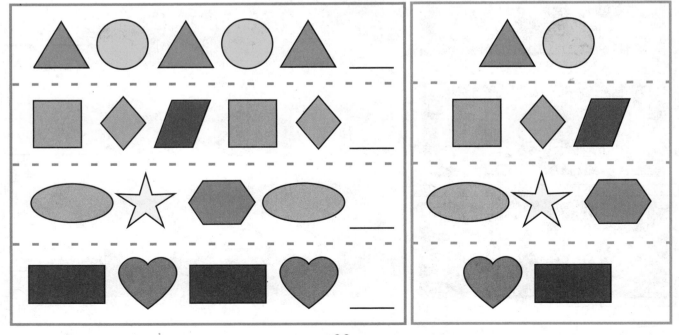

26

1 **Match the shape to its name.**

circle

triangle

octagon

square

oval

rectangle

diamond

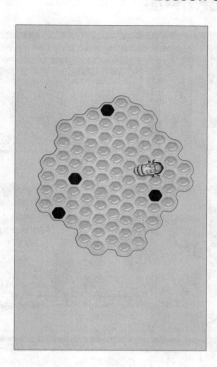

2 **Write the Arabic numbers.**

I	II	III	IV	V	VI	VII	VIII	IX	X	L	C	D	M
1	2	3	4	5	6	7	8	9	10	50	100	500	1,000

VII = _____   IV = _____   IX = _____

XV = _____   XVI = _____   III = _____

XIII = _____   XX = _____   XIX = _____

3 **Multiply to find the product.**

X	2	3	5
6			
4			
8			

X	1	3	10
5			
2			
7			

X	0	2	5
3			
9			
0			

27

4 **Write the value.**

  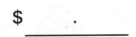

$ _____ .

$ _____ .

$ _____ .

5 **Write the numbers.**

6 hundreds + 2 tens = _____ hundreds + 12 tens

4 hundreds + 8 tens = _____ hundreds + 18 tens

7 hundreds + 5 tens = _____ hundreds + 15 tens

3 hundreds + 1 ten = _____ hundreds + 11 tens

5 hundreds + 0 tens = _____ hundreds + 10 tens

6 **Circle the next shape in sequence.**

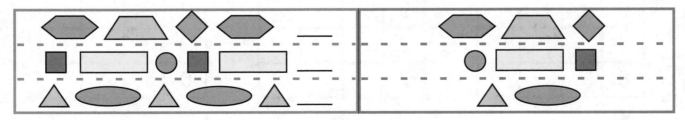

1 Put an X on the money needed.

$ 2.35

$ 5.66

$ 6.83

2 Write the Roman numerals.

I	V	X	XX	XXX	XL	L	LX	LXX	LXXX	XC	C	D	M
1	5	10	20	30	40	50	60	70	80	90	100	500	1,000

46 = 40 + 6 = _____   38 = 30 + 8 = _____

62 = 60 + 2 = _____   71 = 70 + 1 = _____

27 = 20 + 7 = _____   13 = 10 + 3 = _____

54 = 50 + 4 = _____   85 = 80 + 5 = _____

90 = 90 + 0 = _____   29   100 = 100 + 0 = _____

3 **Circle the next shape in sequence.**

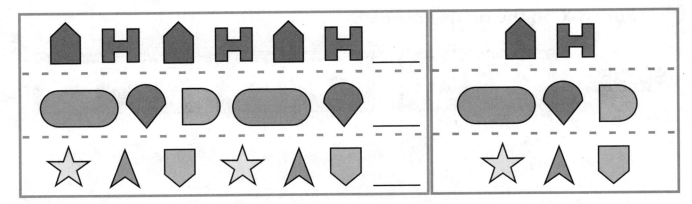

4 **Write the numbers.**

$7 + \underline{\quad} = 16$
$\underline{\quad} - 8 = 5$
$\underline{\quad} - 4 = 1$
$\underline{\quad} + 8 = 13$

$\underline{\quad} + 3 = 4$
$10 - \underline{\quad} = 1$
$4 + \underline{\quad} = 5$
$\underline{\quad} - 7 = 7$

$8 - \underline{\quad} = 5$
$\underline{\quad} + 6 = 11$
$6 + \underline{\quad} = 13$
$\underline{\quad} + 8 = 17$

5 **Match the shape to its name.**

 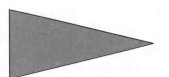  

square   circle   rectangle   oval   octagon   triangle   diamond

6 **Multiply to find the product.**

X	2	7	5	8	1	0	6	10	3	9	4
5											
3											

① **Write the name of each shape.**

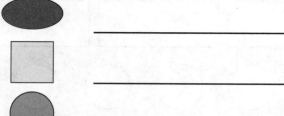

_____

_____

_____

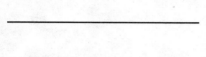

_____

_____

② **Match the Roman numerals to the Arabic numbers.**

II	18	XC	14
LXXV	81	XXXIII	6
XVIII	75	VI	57
IX	2	XIV	90
LXXXI	9	LVII	33

③ **Write the numbers.**

2 - ____ = 2	7 - ____ = 0	____ - 4 = 2
____ + 1 = 9	6 + ____ = 10	16 - ____ = 8
____ - 9 = 2	____ + 0 = 5	2 + ____ = 4
5 + ____ = 7	____ - 5 = 6	____ + 5 = 12
9 + ____ = 12	9 - ____ = 7	____ + 7 = 15

31

4 **Write the value needed on the money.**

$ 3.42

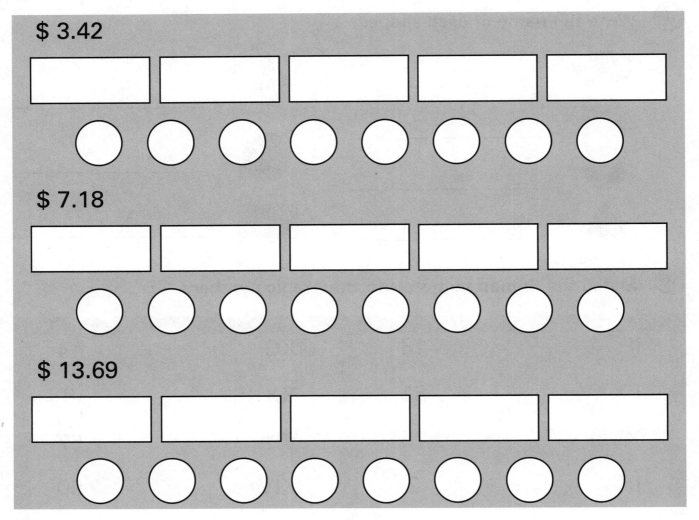

$ 7.18

$ 13.69

5 Burk Street has 43 houses on it. Gilbert Road has 61 houses on it. Burk Street has how many less houses than Gilbert?

Anita made 68 snowballs behind her fort. Stan made 84 snowballs behind his fort. Anita made how many less snowballs than Stan?

1 **Subtract to find the difference.**

$\overset{4\ 1}{\cancel{5}}04$ $-\ 211$ 293	$\overset{6\ 1}{\cancel{7}}05$ $-\ 461$ 244	305 $-\ 245$	705 $-\ 673$	604 $-\ 323$	802 $-\ 441$	607 $-\ 451$

604 $-\ 192$	704 $-\ 524$	807 $-\ 133$	608 $-\ 252$	307 $-\ 177$	508 $-\ 463$	607 $-\ 512$

2 **Write the numbers.**

three 6's = ___ + ___ + ___ = ___ x ___ = ___

four 6's = ___ + ___ + ___ + ___ = ___ x ___ = ___

two 6's = ___ + ___ = ___ x ___ = ___

eight 6's = ___ + ___ + ___ + ___ + ___ + ___ + ___ + ___ = ___ x ___ = ___

five 6's = ___ + ___ + ___ + ___ + ___ = ___ x ___ = ___

nine 6's = ___ + ___ + ___ + ___ + ___ + ___ + ___ + ___ + ___ = ___ x ___ = ___

six 6's = ___ + ___ + ___ + ___ + ___ + ___ = ___ x ___ = ___

seven 6's = ___ + ___ + ___ + ___ + ___ + ___ + ___ = ___ x ___ = ___

3 **Write the Roman numerals.**

37	_____		59	_____
63	_____		78	_____
15	_____		42	_____
24	_____		96	_____

4 **Write the letter on the shape.**

square - S

rectangle - R

triangle - T

circle - C

oval - O

octagon - E

diamond - D

5 **Circle the hidden word numbers:**

1, 2, 3, 6, 7, 8, 10, 11, 14, 19, 22, 41, 50, 56, 60, 74, 83

F	S	S	F	S	S	N	F	I	F	T	Y	–	O	Y
I	L	E	O	E	I	G	H	T	O	–	T	H	R	E
F	T	V	U	V	X	–	F	O	R	T	W	O	–	S
T	Y	E	R	E	T	W	E	N	T	Y	–	T	W	O
Y	–	L	T	N	Y	–	N	O	Y	S	T	H	Y	N
–	F	E	E	I	G	H	T	Y	–	T	H	R	E	E
S	E	V	E	N	T	Y	–	F	O	U	R	E	E	W
I	H	E	N	G	H	–	T	E	N	–	T	E	N	T
X	T	N	N	I	N	E	T	E	E	N	–	S	I	X

34

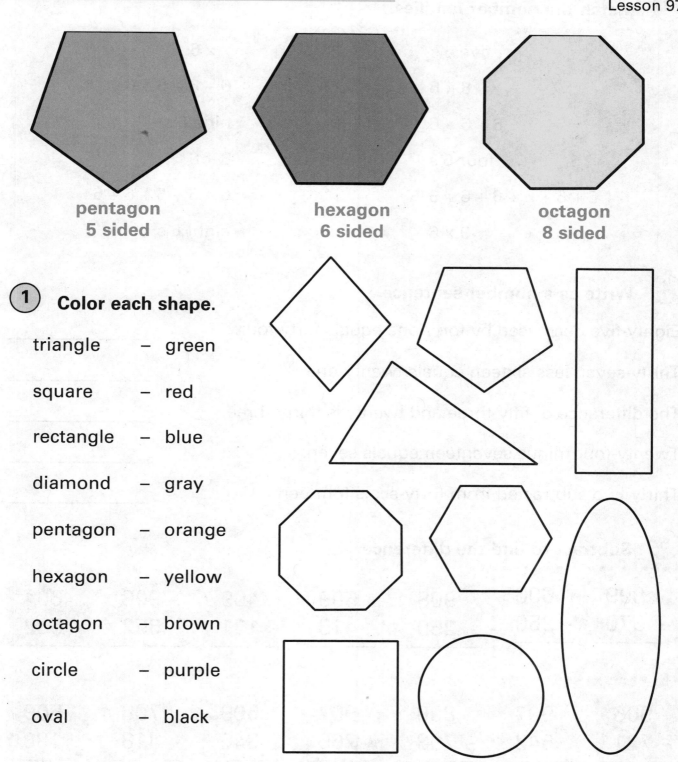

pentagon
5 sided

hexagon
6 sided

octagon
8 sided

① **Color each shape.**

triangle   – green

square   – red

rectangle   – blue

diamond   – gray

pentagon   – orange

hexagon   – yellow

octagon   – brown

circle   – purple

oval   – black

② February has 28 days except for leap year. July has 31 days. February usually has how many less days than July?

35

③ Match the number families.

five 6's	7 x 6
8 x 6	6 + 6 + 6 + 6
6 + 6 + 6	nine 6's
four 6's	3 x 6
6 + 6 + 6 + 6 + 6 + 6 + 6	6 + 6 + 6 + 6 + 6
9 x 6	eight 6's

④ Write as a number sentence.

Eighty-five decreased by forty-one equals forty-four.   _____

Thirty-seven less sixteen equals twenty-one.   _____

The difference of fifty-three and twenty is thirty-three.   _____

Twenty-four minus seventeen equals seven.   _____

Thirty-two subtracted from forty-six is fourteen.   _____

⑤ Subtract to find the difference.

$$\begin{array}{r} ^{7\ 1}\!\!\not{8}09 \\ -\ 570 \\ \hline \end{array} \qquad \begin{array}{r} ^{5\ 1}\!\!\not{6}06 \\ -\ 250 \\ \hline \end{array}$$

908	509	409	908	604
- 250	- 419	- 121	- 352	- 532

906	907	806	907	509	708	509
- 721	- 542	- 793	- 265	- 346	- 418	- 188

36

1 **Family Members**

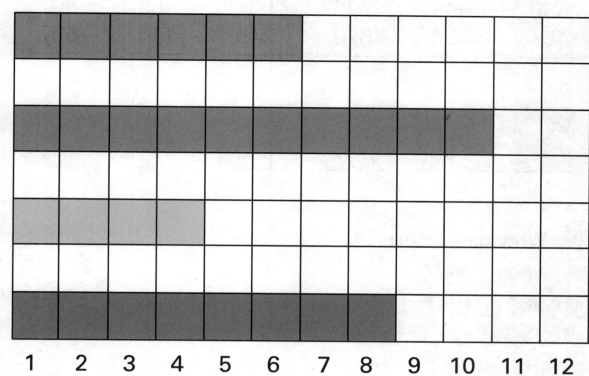

Janice

Jerry

Joyce

John

1 2 3 4 5 6 7 8 9 10 11 12

How many people are in Joyce's family? _____

How many people are in Janice's family? _____

How many people are in John's family? _____

How many people are in Jerry's family? _____

Which family is the largest? _____

Which family is the smallest? _____

2 **Find the sum. Write even or odd.**

243 _____
+ 685 _____
_____

564 _____
+ 172 _____
_____

326 _____
+ 457 _____
_____

37

3 Subtract to find the difference.

609	908	906	908	409	807	908
- 481	- 754	- 670	- 245	- 114	- 637	- 567

205	704	803	703	906	304	809
- 182	- 650	- 121	- 343	- 674	- 293	- 363

4 Write the numbers.

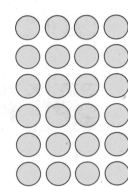

_____ rows of _____ = _____

_____ x _____ = _____

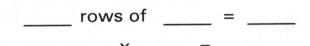

_____ rows of _____ = _____

_____ x _____ = _____

_____ rows of _____ = _____

_____ x _____ = _____

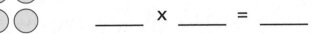

_____ rows of _____ = _____

_____ x _____ = _____

5 Write the name pentagon, hexagon, or octagon on the correct shape.

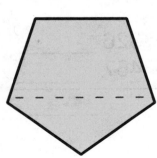

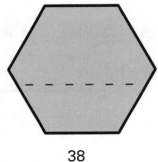

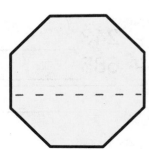

38

1 Money in the Bank

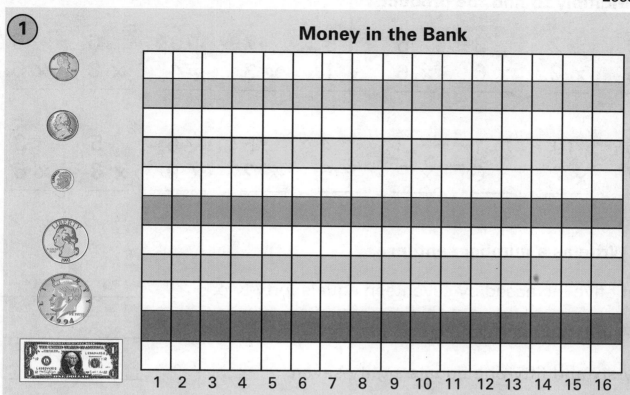

Color the blocks for:

11 pennies   5 quarters   8 nickels   14 dimes

4 half dollars   1 dollar bill

2 Find the difference.

304	206	504	601	603	507	406
- 242	- 171	- 413	- 280	- 453	- 234	- 195

807	702	508	702	307	705	608
- 321	- 350	- 371	- 632	- 145	- 261	- 382

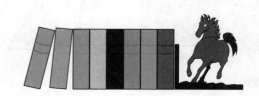

3 Multiply to find the product.

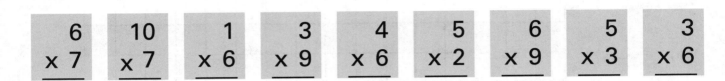

| 0 x 5 | 2 x 6 | 3 x 8 | 5 x 6 | 8 x 1 | 7 x 3 | 10 x 4 | 6 x 8 | 6 x 6 |

| 6 x 7 | 10 x 7 | 1 x 6 | 3 x 9 | 4 x 6 | 5 x 2 | 6 x 9 | 5 x 3 | 3 x 6 |

4 Write as a number sentence.

Twenty-five increased by seventeen equals forty-two.   _____

Forty-eight plus thirteen equals sixty-one.   _____

Thirty-six and fifty-one equals eighty-seven.   _____

Eight added to thirty-four is forty-two.   _____

5 Find the sum. Write even or odd.

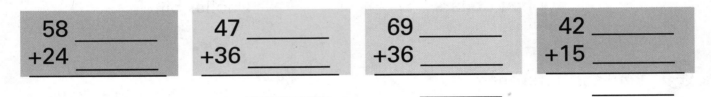

| 58 _____ +24 _____ _____ | 47 _____ +36 _____ _____ | 69 _____ +36 _____ _____ | 42 _____ +15 _____ _____ |

6 Match one half to the other half.

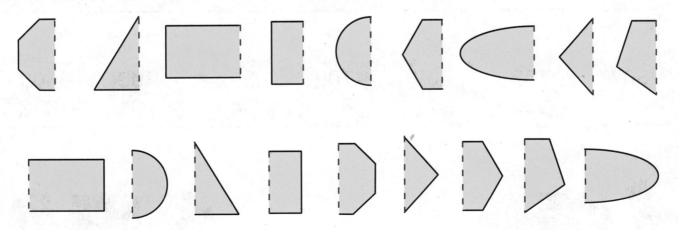

1 **Circle the next shape in sequence.**   **3 pts.**

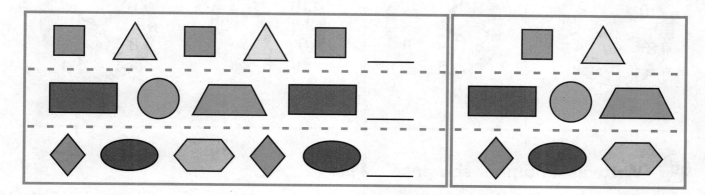

2 **Write the fraction that shows what part is shaded.**   **4 pts.**

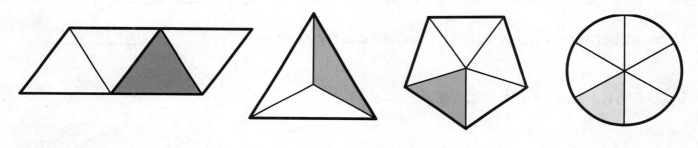

_____   _____   _____   _____

3 **Write the numbers.**   **20 pts.**

6 thousands + 5 hundreds + 3 tens + 7 ones = ____ + ____ + ____ + ____ = ____

4 thousands + 7 hundreds + 1 ten + 6 ones = ____ + ____ + ____ + ____ = ____

8 thousands + 9 hundreds + 4 tens + 2 ones = ____ + ____ + ____ + ____ = ____

2 thousands + 6 hundreds + 8 tens + 5 ones = ____ + ____ + ____ + ____ = ____

4 **Find the sum. Write even or odd.**   **12 pts.**

75 _____	38 _____	19 _____	22 _____
+24 _____	+46 _____	+51 _____	+35 _____
_____	_____	_____	_____

⑤ Write the correct time. 4 pts.

_____ : _____   _____ : _____   _____ : _____   _____ : _____

⑥ Write as a number sentence. 3 pts.

Twenty-five minus twelve equals thirteen.   _____

Fifty-one decreased by thirty-six is fifteen.   _____

Nine subtracted from thirty equals twenty-one.   _____

⑦ Write the numbers. 9 pts.

16 - ___ = 7	15 - ___ = 7	7 + ___ = 11
___ + 6 = 14	8 + ___ = 13	___ + 3 = 3
___ - 9 = 4	11 - ___ = 2	6 + ___ = 15

⑧

Julia read a book with 264 pages. Joy's book had 238 pages. Joy's book had how many fewer pages than Julia's?

There were 386 students in Kathy's high school. David's high school had 269 students. David's high school had how many fewer students than Kathy's?

2 pts.

1 Find the sum.

| ☐ 3,902 +5,436 | ☐ 7,531 +1,546 | ☐ 2,824 +6,723 | ☐ 4,210 +3,870 | ☐ 5,617 +3,812 | ☐ 3,851 +2,348 |

| ☐ 4,741 +1,703 | ☐ 5,467 +1,630 | ☐ 2,906 +4,912 | ☐ 6,728 +1,931 | ☐ 1,530 +4,919 | ☐ 4,136 +2,930 |

2 Write = or ≠.

 _____ pentagon

_____ triangle

 _____ oval

 _____ diamond

 _____ rectangle

 _____ oval

 _____ hexagon

 _____ rectangle

 _____ octagon

3 Find the difference.

| 919 - 238 | 868 - 690 | 829 - 753 | 947 - 587 | 919 - 769 | 938 - 474 | 907 - 367 |

| 879 - 596 | 624 - 184 | 549 - 270 | | 867 - 480 | 639 - 481 | 456 - 286 |

43

4 **Make a bar graph from the picture below.**

Animals in the Barnyard

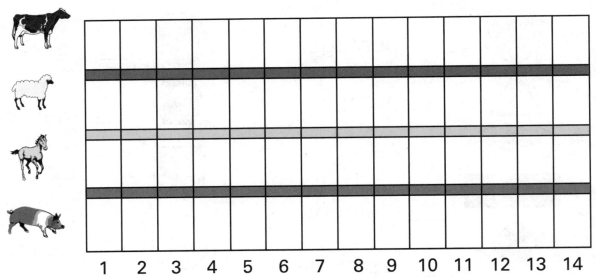

| | 1 | 2 | 3 | 4 | 5 | 6 | 7 | 8 | 9 | 10 | 11 | 12 | 13 | 14 |

5 **Multiply to find the product.**

4	3	9	1	7	3	6	7	3
x 6	x 3	x 3	x 6	x 6	x 5	x 6	x 2	x 6

3	2	1	8	8	6	8	9	0
x 2	x 6	x 4	x 6	x 3	x 5	x 2	x 6	x 6

44

1 Write the correct time.

_____ : _____   _____ : _____   _____ : _____   _____ : _____

2 Multiply to find the product.

0 x 7	6 x 3	9 x 2	3 x 7	6 x 5	2 x 3	9 x 6	2 x 4	6 x 0

| 10 <br> x 9 | 3 <br> x 8 | 6 <br> x 1 | 4 <br> x 3 | 8 <br> x 6 | 0 <br> x 8 | 10 <br> x 3 | 6 <br> x 4 | 8 <br> x 1 |

| 2 <br> x 7 | 6 <br> x 6 | 5 <br> x 3 | 10 <br> x 7 | 4 <br> x 5 | 6 <br> x 2 | 3 <br> x 9 | 4 <br> x 1 | 7 <br> x 6 |

3 Write the numbers.

1 + _____ = 5	16 - _____ = 8	_____ - 5 = 4
_____ - 0 = 2	13 - _____ = 9	_____ + 8 = 17
8 + _____ = 15	_____ - 8 = 5	6 - _____ = 2
_____ - 1 = 4	14 - _____ = 8	_____ + 9 = 16
2 + _____ = 5	_____ + 6 = 12	8 - _____ = 5

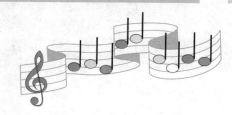 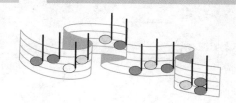

4 Find the difference.

614 - 231	849 - 751	708 - 653	934 - 763	757 - 465	759 - 179	329 - 298

238 - 155	925 - 464	637 - 597	965 - 370	945 - 593	713 - 363	608 - 386

5 Find the sum.

4,736 +3,632	1,354 +7,824	3,652 +4,834	2,874 +6,315	2,463 +3,915	1,527 +5,750

4,273 +1,922	3,586 +1,913	1,925 +6,474	1,482 +2,702	4,819 +2,830	2,953 +1,916

6 Write = or ≠.

3 + 3 ____ 15 - 8   5 + 1 ____ 14 - 8   1 + 0 ____ 8 - 8

9 - 0 ____ 9 + 4   11 - 8 ____ 7 + 0   14 - 7 ____ 4 + 3

5 + 4 ____ 18 - 9   4 + 2 ____ 10 - 4   9 + 6 ____ 4 - 1

9 - 6 ____ 3 + 1   9 - 2 ____ 5 + 2   8 - 6 ____ 9 - 4

1 **Write the numbers.**

4,861 = _____ + _____ + _____ + _____   6,153 = _____ + _____ + _____ + _____

2,573 = _____ + _____ + _____ + _____   2,709 = _____ + _____ + _____ + _____

9,804 = _____ + _____ + _____ + _____   1,645 = _____ + _____ + _____ + _____

2 **Write = or ≠.**

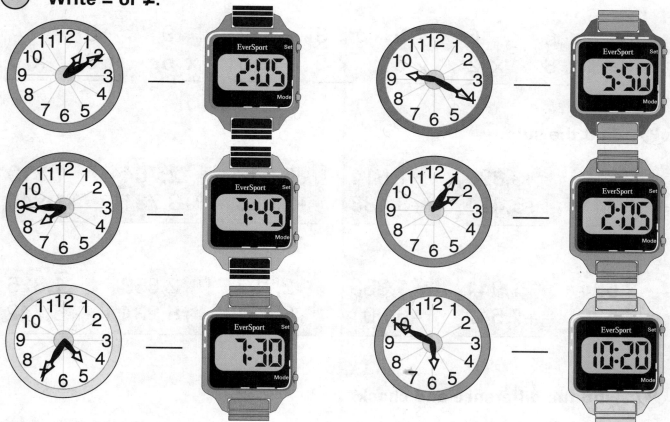

3 **Write the numbers.**

_____ + 7 = 9	16 - _____ = 9	10 - _____ = 5
12 - _____ = 3	9 + _____ = 15	_____ + 3 = 7
_____ - 9 = 4	_____ + 5 = 8	1 + _____ = 9
7 + _____ = 14	14 - _____ = 7	_____ - 6 = 2
8 + _____ = 17	_____ - 2 = 0	_____ + 8 = 14

4. Multiply to find the product.

4 × 5	8 × 6	3 × 5	6 × 0	8 × 3	8 × 1	3 × 3	10 × 3	1 × 3
4 × 3	6 × 4	7 × 5	10 × 6	3 × 7	5 × 6	5 × 5	3 × 2	6 × 1
6 × 3	5 × 8	6 × 2	10 × 5	3 × 9	9 × 6	9 × 5	0 × 3	4 × 0

5. Find the sum.

5,212 +1,841	3,820 +5,421	1,614 +3,483	6,943 +2,826	2,764 +3,731	1,810 +1,946
3,534 +1,520	1,941 +7,542	1,358 +6,901	2,707 +6,431	2,653 +5,934	1,825 +5,742

6. Find the difference and check.

975 - 681	713 - 491	238 - 145	619 - 272	958 - 391	324 - 274	412 - 182
618 - 327	748 - 262	819 - 250	629 - 547	718 - 534	518 - 340	425 - 234

1 Write the fraction that shows what part is shaded.

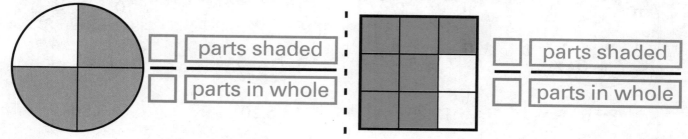

	parts shaded
	parts in whole

	parts shaded
	parts in whole

	parts shaded
	parts in whole

	parts shaded
	parts in whole

	parts shaded
	parts in whole

	parts shaded
	parts in whole

2 Write the numbers.

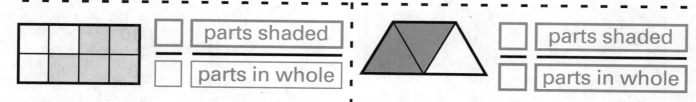

1,538 = _____ + _____ + _____ + _____   3,491 = _____ + _____ + _____ + _____

4,269 = _____ + _____ + _____ + _____   6,527 = _____ + _____ + _____ + _____

7,085 = _____ + _____ + _____ + _____   5,642 = _____ + _____ + _____ + _____

3 Find the difference and check.

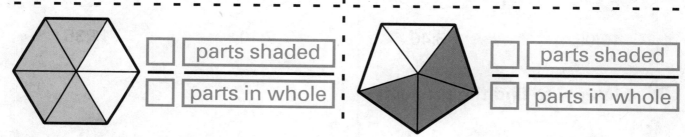

729	816	945	429	359	817	935
- 658	- 634	- 461	- 382	- 185	- 293	- 685

608	634	967	807	415	748	676
- 173	- 254	- 182	- 521	- 362	- 290	- 390

4 Draw both hands on the clocks.

8:55   12:25   6:20   3:50

10:05   5:40   7:10   11:35

5 Multiply to find the product.

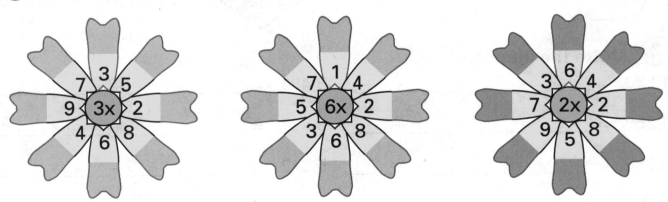

6 Find the sum.

6,714	1,620	3,501	7,723	3,564	2,314
+2,860	+7,672	+4,646	+1,526	+2,801	+3,723

5,423	5,911	3,723	1,940	3,812	5,923
+2,860	+3,658	+1,313	+4,247	+2,535	+ 145

1 There were four vases on the table. Each vase had 3 flowers in it. How many flowers are there in all?

_____ x _____ = _____ _____

Jason has five packs of pens with six pens in each pack. How many pens does Jason have?

_____ x _____ = _____ _____

Mother bought 7 oranges at 10¢ an orange. What did the oranges cost Mother?

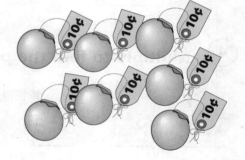

_____ x _____ = _____ _____

2 **Find the difference and check.**

978	457	739	658	847	528	836
- 281	- 291	- 649	- 361	- 354	- 237	- 274

719	649	704	519	863	626	509
- 383	- 278	- 591	- 346	- 592	- 576	- 134

③ Write the fraction that shows what part is shaded.

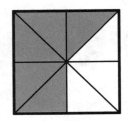   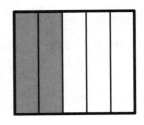   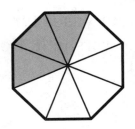   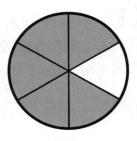

___   ___   ___   ___

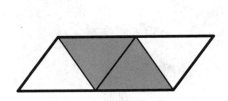      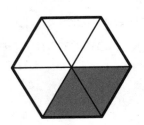   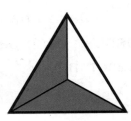

___   ___   ___   ___

④ Multiply to find the product.

6	3	2	7	6	5	6	0	3
x 6	x 4	x 6	x 3	x 5	x 4	x 9	x 6	x 3

8	7	6	10	8	6	9	3	6
x 6	x 5	x 1	x 6	x 1	x 3	x 0	x 9	x 7

⑤ Find the sum.

4,712	4,816	7,423	4,981	2,636	4,821
+2,943	+1,651	+1,621	+3,706	+4,722	+4,751

5,730	1,952	2,681	5,717	3,162	3,851
+1,456	+3,347	+1,518	+3,522	+4,936	+ 227

52

① **Write the ratio.**

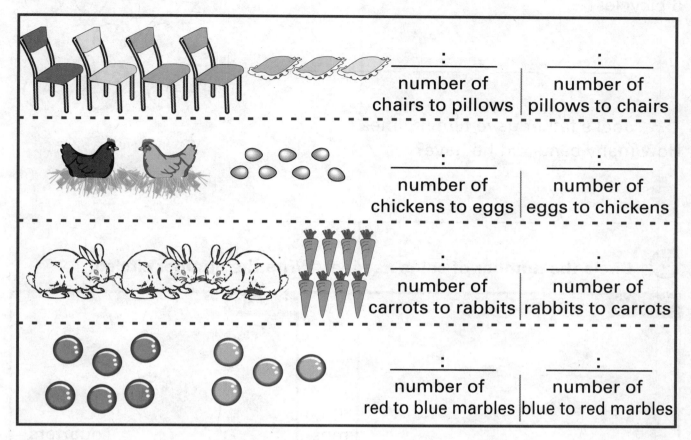

:	:
number of chairs to pillows	number of pillows to chairs

:	:
number of chickens to eggs	number of eggs to chickens

:	:
number of carrots to rabbits	number of rabbits to carrots

:	:
number of red to blue marbles	number of blue to red marbles

② **Multiply to find the product.**

X	3	1	6	9	0	10	4	7	2	8	5
3											

X	4	2	9	6	3	10	1	8	7	0	5
6											

③ **Find the difference and check.**

835	953	486	824	937	663	849
- 494	- 771	- 392	- 690	- 162	- 173	- 385

4 6 bicycles were parked at the store. Each had 2 wheels. How many wheels were on the 6 bicycles?

_____ x _____ = _____ _____

Joel's father gave him 5 dimes. How many cents did he have?

_____ x _____ = _____ _____

5 **Circle the number of coins needed. Write the number circled.**

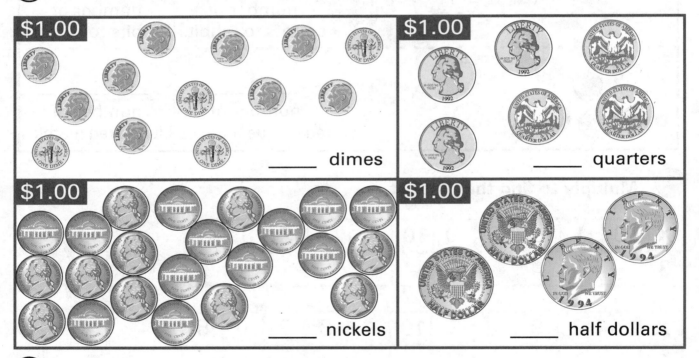

$1.00   _____ dimes

$1.00   _____ quarters

$1.00   _____ nickels

$1.00   _____ half dollars

6 **Write the fraction that shows what part is shaded.**

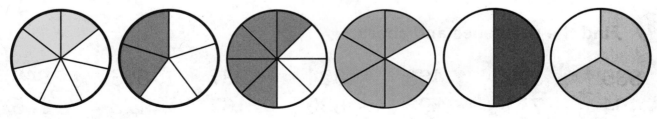

____   ____   ____   ____   ____   ____

1 **Write the ratio.**

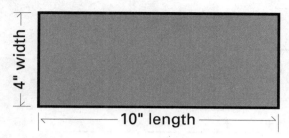

length to width   ___ : ___

width to length   ___ : ___

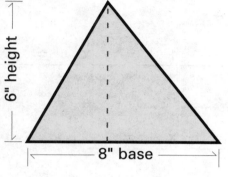

base to height   ___ : ___

height to base   ___ : ___

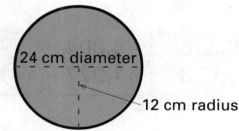

diameter to radius   ___ : ___

radius to diameter   ___ : ___

2 How many dimes do you need to equal one dollar?   ___

How many quarters do you need to equal one dollar?   ___

How many nickels do you need to equal one dollar?   ___

How many pennies do you need to equal one dollar?   ___

How many half dollars do you need to equal one dollar?   ___

3 Josh had 2 ice cream cones. There were 3 dips on each cone. How many dips of ice cream did he have?

___ x ___ = ___ _____

4 **Write the numbers.**

three 9's = ___ + ___ + ___ = ___ x ___ = ___

four 9's = ___ + ___ + ___ + ___ = ___ x ___ = ___

two 9's = ___ + ___ = ___ x ___ = ___

eight 9's = ___ + ___ + ___ + ___ + ___ + ___ + ___ + ___ = ___ x ___ = ___

five 9's = ___ + ___ + ___ + ___ + ___ = ___ x ___ = ___

nine 9's = ___ + ___ + ___ + ___ + ___ + ___ + ___ + ___ + ___ = ___ x ___ = ___

six 9's = ___ + ___ + ___ + ___ + ___ + ___ = ___ x ___ = ___

seven 9's = ___ + ___ + ___ + ___ + ___ + ___ + ___ = ___ x ___ = ___

5 **Find the sum.**

1,205	3,963	6,628	5,316	4,804	7,719
+1,846	+4,517	+2,426	+1,978	+1,277	+1,631

6 **Write 2 addition and 2 subtraction facts.**

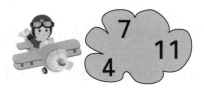

15
9   6

7
4   11

5
8   13

_____   _____   _____

_____   _____   _____

_____   _____   _____

_____   _____   _____

7 **Write < or >.**

17 - 9 ___ 6   16 - 7 ___ 7   13 - 4 ___ 10

11 - 3 ___ 9   12 - 5 ___ 6

56

$$4 + n = 9 \qquad 6 + n = 13 \qquad 5 + n = 14$$
$$-4 \qquad -4 \qquad\quad -6 \qquad -6 \qquad\quad -5 \qquad -5$$
$$n = 5 \qquad\qquad n = 7 \qquad\qquad n = 9$$

1 Solve the equations.

$2 + n = 11$	$7 + n = 15$	$3 + n = 6$	$4 + n = 13$
$1 + n = 8$	$5 + n = 10$	$5 + n = 7$	$9 + n = 12$

2 Find the sum.

1,509	2,821	3,923	1,506	4,426	5,738
+4,587	+5,849	+2,218	+6,759	+3,865	+3,713

3 Find the difference.

5,321	4,513	6,265	3,412	6,735	2,654
- 4,161	- 1,362	- 2,182	- 3,340	- 1,441	- 2,392

4 Write < or >.

6 x 9 ___ 63   9 x 9 ___ 72   3 x 9 ___ 18

4 x 9 ___ 45   8 x 9 ___ 81   7 x 9 ___ 54

57

5 **Write the value.**

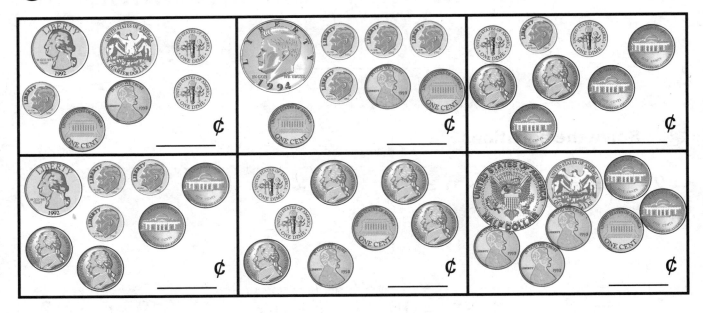

6 **Write the ratio.**

The number of triangles to the number of squares   ___ : ___

The number of squares to the number of triangles   ___ : ___

The number of triangles to the number of squares and triangles   ___ : ___

The number of squares to the number of triangles and squares   ___ : ___

7 **Match the number families.**

six 9's	eight 9's
9 + 9 + 9 + 9	9 + 9 + 9 + 9 + 9
8 x 9	9 + 9 + 9 + 9 + 9 + 9
5 x 9	four 9's

1 **Write the Roman numerals.**

I	IV	V	IX	X	XL	L	XC	C	CD	D	CM	M
1	4	5	9	10	40	50	90	100	400	500	900	1,000

7 _____

13 _____

29 _____

48 _____

52 _____

61 _____

74 _____

82 _____

95 _____

105 _____

2 **Find the difference.**

9,877 - 9,382	7,948 - 5,882	7,809 - 6,157	8,936 - 4,696	8,926 - 6,445	9,718 - 5,085

3 **Solve the equations.**

$4 + n = 8$ $- 4 \quad\quad -4$ _____ $\quad\quad n =$	$5 + n = 14$	$6 + n = 7$	$7 + n = 11$
$5 + n = 11$	$4 + n = 10$	$8 + n = 12$	$2 + n = 10$

4 Match the pairs of multiplication facts.

6 x 9	7 x 9	3 x 9	7 x 9
2 x 9	9 x 2	9 x 7	4 x 9
9 x 7	9 x 6	9 x 8	9 x 3
5 x 9	9 x 5	9 x 4	8 x 9

5 Find the sum.

6,784	4,857	3,542	1,826	1,937	1,809
+1,806	+4,923	+5,829	+2,536	+5,439	+1,428

6 Write the value.

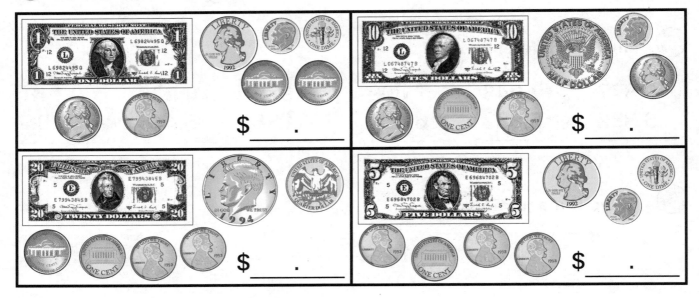

$ ____ . ____

$ ____ . ____

$ ____ . ____

$ ____ . ____

7 Shade the shape for each fractional part.

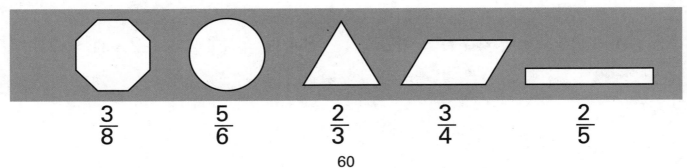

$\frac{3}{8}$ $\frac{5}{6}$ $\frac{2}{3}$ $\frac{3}{4}$ $\frac{2}{5}$

Number of Points Made by Ken in Basketball

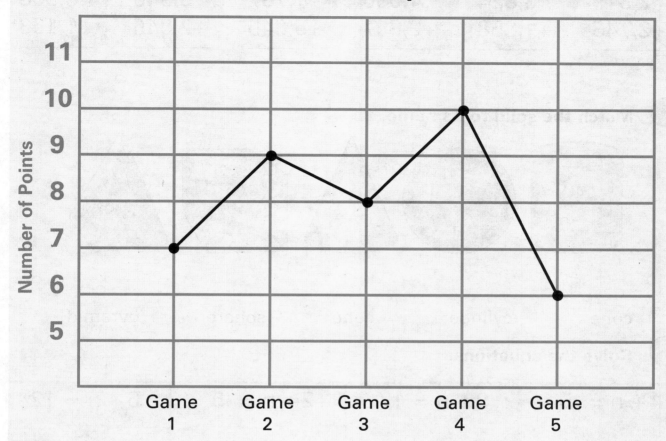

① How many points did Ken score in game 1? _____

How many points did Ken score in game 3? _____

In what game did he score the most points? _____

In what game did he score the least points? _____

How many points did he score in games 2 and 4? _____

② **Find the difference.**

6,739	8,757	6,429	4,577	9,315	2,648
- 4,153	- 8,387	- 5,232	- 3,195	- 1,170	- 1,097

3 **Find the sum.**

| 2,319 +2,743 | 3,824 +1,858 | 4,636 +2,857 | 1,707 +5,845 | 5,945 +2,846 | 6,908 +1,153 |

4 **Match the solid to its name.**

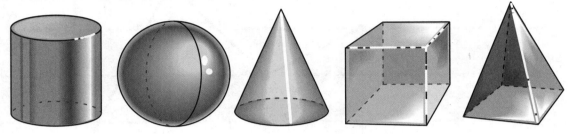

cone   cylinder   cube   sphere   pyramid

5 **Solve the equations.**

4 + n = 5	9 + n = 17	2 + n = 5	6 + n = 12
8 + n = 15	3 + n = 10	7 + n = 16	7 + n = 12

6 **Write the answers.**

Is 23 closer to 20 or 30? _____   Is 62 closer to 60 or 70? _____

Is 51 closer to 50 or 60? _____   Is 38 closer to 30 or 40? _____

Is 87 closer to 80 or 90? _____   Is 46 closer to 40 or 50? _____

7 **Shade the shape for each fractional part.**

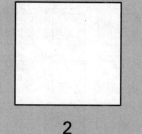

$\frac{2}{4}$

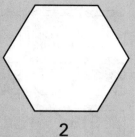

$\frac{2}{6}$

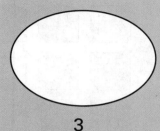

$\frac{3}{4}$

$\frac{3}{7}$

$\frac{5}{6}$

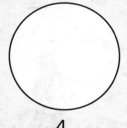

$\frac{4}{5}$

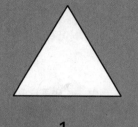

$\frac{1}{2}$

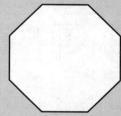

$\frac{7}{8}$

$\frac{3}{8}$

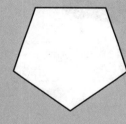

$\frac{3}{5}$

$\frac{5}{9}$

$\frac{4}{6}$

8 **Write the Arabic numbers.**

LXXV = _____   LXXXIV = _____

XXXIII = _____   XLVII = _____

XIX = _____   LX = _____

LI = _____   XCIX = _____

VIII = _____   LXVI = _____

XXVI = _____   II = _____

63

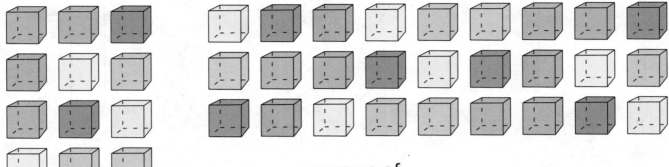

9 **Write the numbers.**

_____ rows of _____ = _____

_____ x _____ = _____

_____ rows of _____ = _____

_____ x _____ = _____

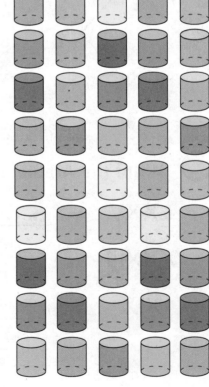

_____ rows of _____ = _____

_____ x _____ = _____

_____ rows of _____ = _____

_____ x _____ = _____

① Correct Spelling Words

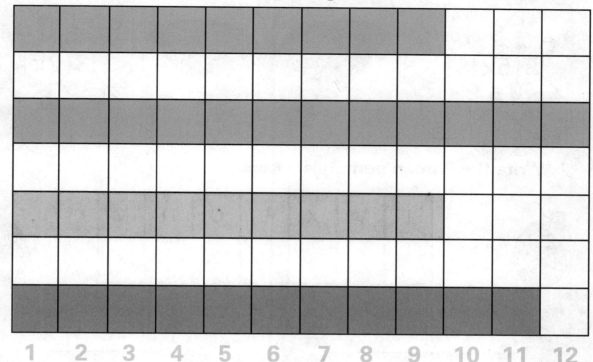

Sue

Peter

Phil

Rose

1 2 3 4 5 6 7 8 9 10 11 12

How many spelling words did Rose get correct? _____

Who spelled the most correct words? _____

What two students spelled the same number correctly? _____

and _____ How many? _____

Which person spelled 12 words correctly? _____   **6 pts.**

② Find the sum. 6 pts.

| 2,118 | 3,545 | 2,053 | 7,254 | 1,325 | 6,470 |
| + 1,790 | + 6,162 | + 6,162 | + 1,672 | + 8,390 | + 1,479 |

③ Bill has 142 pennies in his bank. Ben has 108 pennies in his bank. Ben has how many less pennies than Bill?   **1 pt.**

65

④ Multiply to find the product. 16 pts.

⑤ Write the Roman numerals. 8 pts.

I	V	X	L	C	D	M
1	5	10	50	100	500	1,000

3 _____

9 _____

12 _____

17 _____

21 _____

28 _____

30 _____

36 _____

⑥ Write the fraction that shows what part is shaded. 6 pts.

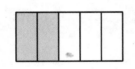    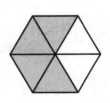

___   ___   ___   ___   ___   ___

⑦ Find the difference and check. 7 pts.

390	691	854	586	782	745	373
- 315	- 353	- 307	- 479	- 204	- 718	- 268

1

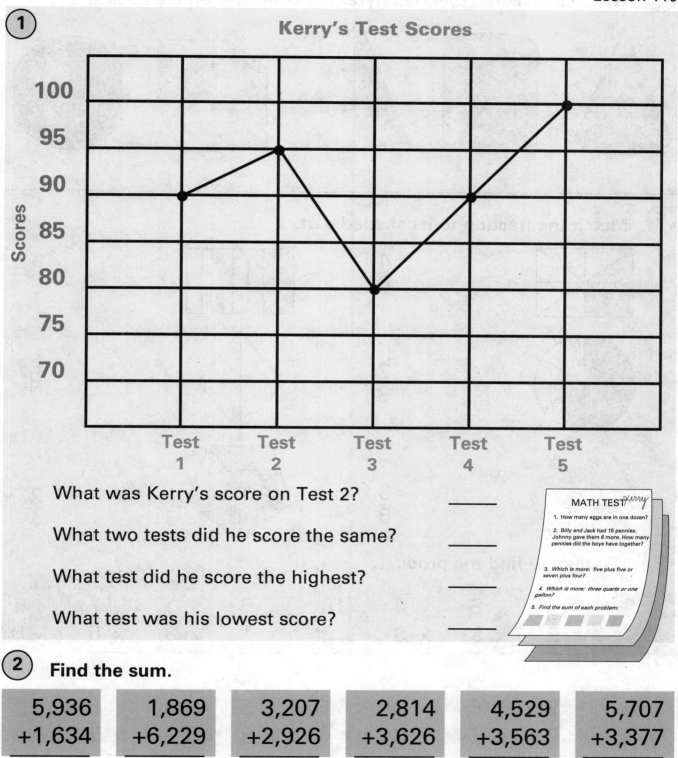

Kerry's Test Scores

What was Kerry's score on Test 2? _____

What two tests did he score the same? _____

What test did he score the highest? _____

What test was his lowest score? _____

MATH TEST *Kerry*

1. How many eggs are in one dozen?

2. Billy and Jack had 15 pennies. Johnny gave them 6 more. How many pennies did the boys have together?

3. Which is more: five plus five or seven plus four?

4. Which is more: three quarts or one gallon?

5. Find the sum of each problem:

2 **Find the sum.**

5,936	1,869	3,207	2,814	4,529	5,707
+1,634	+6,229	+2,926	+3,626	+3,563	+3,377

3 The score at the basketball game was 91-83 at the end of the game. The winning team scored how many more points?

4 Write cube, cone, cylinder, pyramid, or sphere on the lines.

   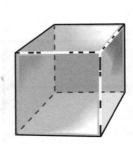 

_____ _____ _____ _____ _____

5 Match the fraction to its shaded part.

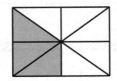 $\frac{4}{6}$ 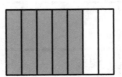 $\frac{4}{5}$

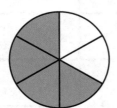 $\frac{2}{3}$ 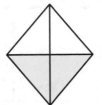 $\frac{5}{7}$

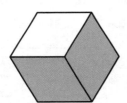 $\frac{3}{8}$ 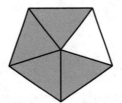 $\frac{2}{4}$

6 Multiply to find the product.

6	9	6	4	10	6	1	7	1
x 4	x 9	x 3	x 9	x 3	x 1	x 3	x 6	x 9

3	2	6	9	6	3	5	3	10
x 5	x 9	x 2	x 8	x 6	x 2	x 9	x 7	x 9

3	3	9	8	8	4	2	6	9
x 3	x 9	x 6	x 3	x 6	x 3	x 8	x 5	x 7

1 **Draw the line on the graph.**

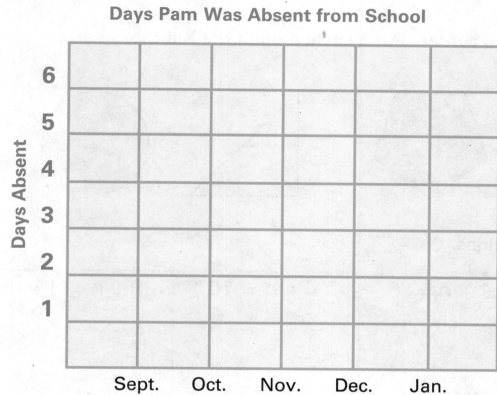

Days Pam Was Absent from School

Month	Days Absent
September	1
October	2
November	1
December	3
January	4

2 **Multiply to find the product.**

6	2	6	9	8	4	6	2	0
x 9	x 9	x 5	x 7	x 6	x 9	x 3	x 6	x 9

10	4	1	9	6	10	6	9	6
x 9	x 6	x 9	x 8	x 1	x 6	x 7	x 3	x 6

3 **Write = or ≠.**

 ____ $\frac{2}{6}$ ____ $\frac{1}{4}$

____ $\frac{7}{16}$ ____ $\frac{5}{8}$

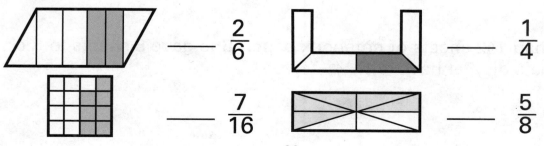

69

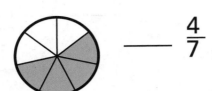 —— $\frac{4}{7}$ 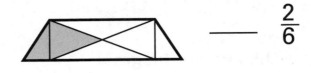 —— $\frac{2}{6}$

4   Put an X on each corner. Put a circle around the X if the corner is square.

      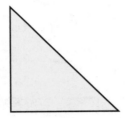 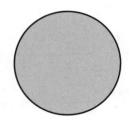

5   Solve the equations.

6 + n = 11	1 + n = 6	4 + n = 10	9 + n = 14
3 + n = 8	8 + n = 14	0 + n = 8	2 + n = 6

6   Find the difference and check.

213	309	429	547	664	438	889
- 193	- 172	- 251	- 363	- 390	- 172	- 493

7   Pat had 142 sheets of notebook paper. She gave 8 sheets to Rick. How many sheets did Pat have left?

1 **Match the fractions.**

$\frac{3}{4}$	two-sevenths	$\frac{1}{6}$	six-ninths
$\frac{2}{7}$	one-half	$\frac{5}{8}$	one-sixth
$\frac{4}{5}$	three-fourths	$\frac{6}{9}$	two-thirds
$\frac{1}{2}$	four-fifths	$\frac{2}{3}$	five-eights

2 **Find the sum.**

1,640	2,251	3,574	1,860	3,784	5,832
+1,682	+1,964	+4,984	+7,398	+1,591	+2,694

3 **Match the shape to its name.**

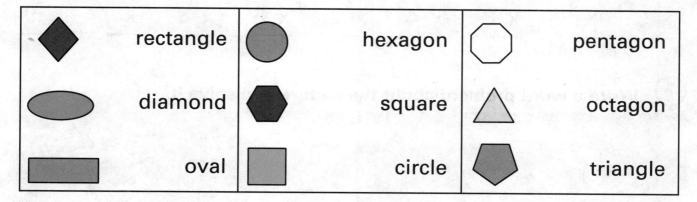

◆	rectangle	●	hexagon	⬡	pentagon
⬭	diamond	⬡	square	△	octagon
▬	oval	■	circle	⬠	triangle

4 **Find the difference and check.**

9,765	8,853	9,648	6,419	4,925	5,337
- 7,575	- 762	- 2,084	- 4,352	- 4,584	- 2,084

5 **Draw the line graph.**

Average Daily Temperature

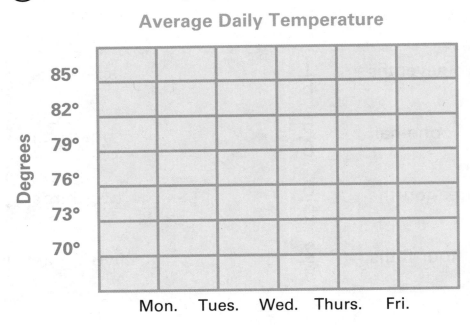

Day	Degrees
Monday	82
Tuesday	79
Wednesday	85
Thursday	82
Friday	76

6 **Multiply to find the product.**

3 x 9	9 x 7	6 x 6	9 x 1	3 x 8	4 x 6	3 x 6	5 x 6	9 x 4

9 x 5	6 x 7	9 x 8	3 x 4	6 x 2	9 x 6	6 x 8	3 x 7	9 x 9

7 **Write a word problem about the picture and solve it.**

_____

_____

1 Write = or ≠.

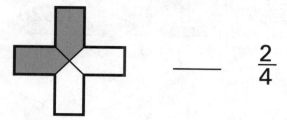 ____ $\dfrac{2}{4}$

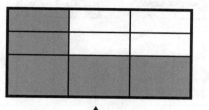 ____ $\dfrac{5}{9}$

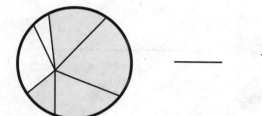 ____ $\dfrac{4}{6}$

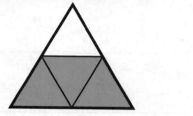 ____ $\dfrac{3}{4}$

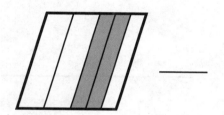 ____ $\dfrac{2}{5}$

____ $\dfrac{7}{8}$

2 Find the sum.

1,696	2,866	1,487	2,930	3,570	5,771
+2,430	+2,473	+5,972	+5,673	+2,769	+ 398

3 Find the sum and circle the correct word.

335 even or odd
+ 183 even or odd
even or odd

682 even or odd
+ 256 even or odd
even or odd

471 even or odd
+ 388 even or odd
even or odd

671 even or odd
+ 248 even or odd
even or odd

even + even = even or odd
even + odd = even or odd
odd + odd = even or odd

73

4 **Find the difference and check.**

7,859	7,824	9,738	6,905	3,846	7,819
- 6,679	- 2,590	- 4,168	- 1,831	- 3,195	- 1,320

5 **Write the name of each shape.**

 _____   _____

 _____   _____

 _____   _____

_____

 _____   _____

6 **Multiply to find the product.**

4	3	9	9	6	3	7	4	6
x 9	x 3	x 5	x 9	x 4	x 9	x 9	x 3	x 3

6	8	7	10	7	9	6	9	10
x 6	x 9	x 3	x 3	x 6	x 2	x 9	x 1	x 6

7 **Write as a number sentence.**

Eight take away five equals three. _____

Nine plus six equals fifteen. _____

Seven increased by four is eleven. _____

Ten decreased by three is seven. _____

1 **Measure the objects in inches.**

_____ _____

_____ _____

_____ _____

2 **Multiply to find the product.**

| 6 × 4 | 4 × 9 | 10 × 6 | 9 × 9 | 3 × 4 | 0 × 9 | 3 × 3 | 6 × 1 | 5 × 9 |

| 6 × 0 | 3 × 6 | 1 × 9 | 8 × 3 | 3 × 2 | 9 × 6 | 6 × 5 | 3 × 9 | 10 × 9 |

3 **Write the even numbers under even and the odd numbers under odd.**

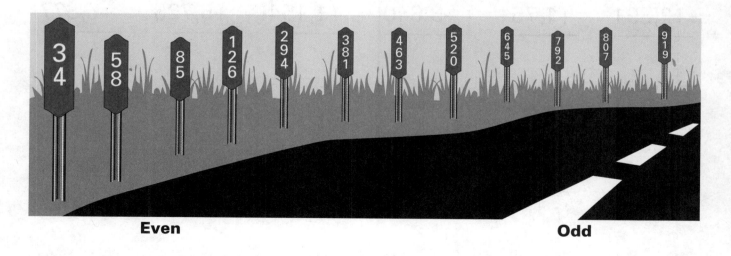

34   58   85   126   294   381   463   520   645   792   807   919

Even   **Odd**

_____ _____ _____   _____ _____ _____

_____ _____ _____   _____ _____ _____

4 **Match the solid to its name.**

cube

cone

cylinder

sphere

pyramid

5 **Write as a number sentence.**

Seven minus one is six. _____

Five subtracted from nine equals four. _____

Three added to ten is thirteen. _____

Eight more than two equals ten. _____

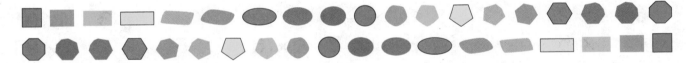

6 **Find the sum.**

6,297	5,958	4,674	6,965	3,780	2,592
+2,891	+1,751	+3,840	+1,154	+5,725	+6,877

7 **Find the difference and check.**

7,917	5,625	5,839	4,706	8,343	9,208
- 3,137	- 2,372	- 5,767	- 3,686	- 4,250	- 4,141

1 **Write the numbers.**

5,000 + 600 + 70 + 4 = _____   4,000 + 200 + 10 + 3 = _____

2,000 + 400 + 30 + 9 = _____   9,000 + 700 + 80 + 1 = _____

7,000 + 800 + 00 + 6 = _____   3,000 + 100 + 50 + 2 = _____

8,000 + 500 + 60 + 5 = _____   6,000 + 300 + 20 + 7 = _____

2 **Write the number of inches for each object. Label the answer.**

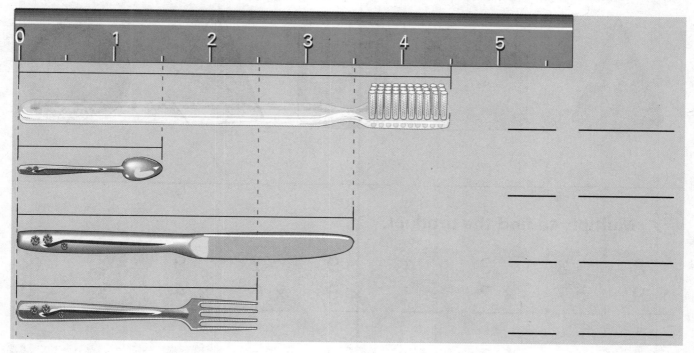

_____ _____

_____ _____

_____ _____

_____ _____

3 **Find the sum.**

1,492	4,792	1,490	3,765	4,871	5,630
+3,783	+2,496	+2,654	+3,841	+3,865	+2,587

2,953	3,853	3,967	4,894	3,581	5,184
+3,670	+1,796	+5,280	+4,915	+2,656	+3,942

4 **Write the next three numbers in the series.**

1	6	9	1	6	___	___	___
4	8	7	4	8	___	___	___
3	5	3	5	3	___	___	___
7	2	0	7	2	___	___	___

5 **Write the name of the solid.**

 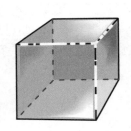   

_____ _____ _____ _____ _____

6 **Multiply to find the product.**

8 x 9	3 x 7	9 x 2	4 x 3	9 x 9	7 x 6	9 x 4	3 x 3	9 x 0

5 x 9	10 x 3	9 x 1	6 x 8	3 x 8	9 x 3	9 x 9	6 x 6	4 x 6

7 **Find the difference and check.**

6,802 - 1,562	4,956 - 1,282	7,714 - 1,562	5,703 - 3,421	9,848 - 6,283	9,573 - 8,190

1 Write the numbers.

three 4's = ___ + ___ + ___ = ___ x ___ = ___

seven 4's = ___ + ___ + ___ + ___ + ___ + ___ + ___ = ___ x ___ = ___

five 4's = ___ + ___ + ___ + ___ + ___ = ___ x ___ = ___

eight 4's = ___ + ___ + ___ + ___ + ___ + ___ + ___ + ___ = ___ x ___ = ___

two 4's = ___ + ___ = ___ x ___ = ___

six 4's = ___ + ___ + ___ + ___ + ___ + ___ = ___ x ___ = ___

four 4's = ___ + ___ + ___ + ___ = ___ x ___ = ___

2 Circle the solid that is different.

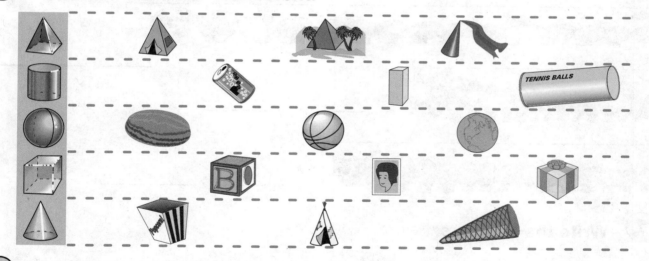

3 Write the next three numbers in the series.

3	5	6	1	3	5	___	___	___
2	7	8	2	7	8	___	___	___
4	0	4	0	4	0	___	___	___
1	9	3	4	1	9	___	___	___

79

(4) **Find the sum.**

| 7,986
+1,232 | 3,765
+4,960 | 2,898
+5,671 | 4,565
+1,573 | 1,894
+7,535 | 6,572
+1,852 |

(5) **Write the numbers.**

7,000 + 100 + 30 + 5 = _____   2,000 + 500 + 60 + 4 = _____

3,000 + 600 + 00 + 1 = _____   9,000 + 300 + 10 + 2 = _____

6,000 + 400 + 70 + 3 = _____   1,000 + 900 + 50 + 9 = _____

8,000 + 200 + 40 + 7 = _____   5,000 + 700 + 20 + 6 = _____

(6) **Measure the objects in inches.**

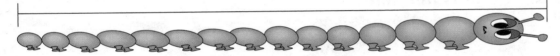

_____ _____

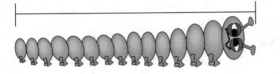

_____ _____

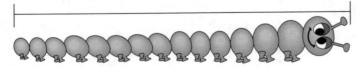

_____ _____

(7) **Write the numbers.**

_____ inches = 1 foot   _____ feet = 1 yard   _____ inches = 1 yard

(8)

John wanted to buy 7 apples at 9¢ each.
How much would the apples cost John?

January	– Jan.		July	
February	– Feb.		August	– Aug.
March	– Mar.		September	– Sept.
April	– Apr.		October	– Oct.
May			November	– Nov.
June			December	– Dec.

1 **Write in the shortened form when possible.**

sixth month _____   second month _____

ninth month _____   twelfth month _____

fifth month _____   third month _____

first month _____   tenth month _____

eleventh month _____   eighth month _____

seventh month _____   fourth month _____

2 **Write the ratio.**

The number of circles to the number of rectangles   ___ : ___

The number of rectangles to the number of pentagons   ___ : ___

The number of circles to the number of pentagons   ___ : ___

The number of pentagons to the number of rectangles   ___ : ___

The number of rectangles to the number of circles   ___ : ___

The number of pentagons to the number of circles   ___ : ___

81

3 **Write the numbers.**

3,000 + 100 + 00 + 5 = _____   4,000 + 600 + 10 + 3 = _____

8,000 + 700 + 60 + 2 = _____   5,000 + 800 + 30 + 7 = _____

4 There were 6 chairs at the table. Each chair had 4 legs. How many chair legs were there altogether?

5 **Measure the objects in inches.**

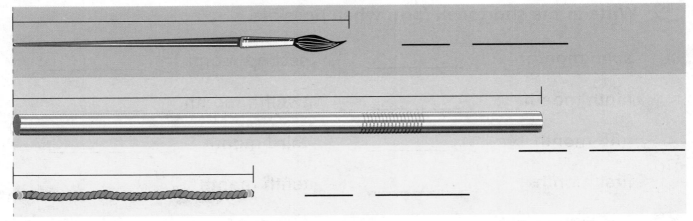

| _____ inches = 1 yard | _____ inches = 1 foot | _____ feet = 1 yard |

6 **Match the number families.**

3 x 4	nine 4's
four 4's	2 x 4
4 + 4 + 4 + 4 + 4	4 + 4 + 4 + 4
six 4's	five 4's
9 x 4	6 x 4
4 + 4	4 + 4 + 4

7 Kay had $36. She wanted to buy a coat for $50. How much more money did she need?

82

①

Number of Mini Cars Owned

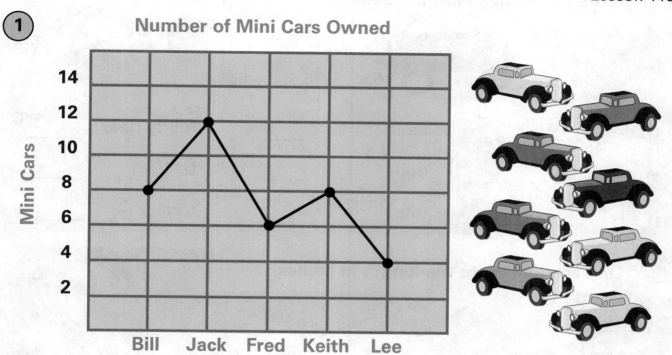

Who has the most mini cars? _____ Who has the least mini cars?

_____ Jack has how many more than Fred? _____ What two boys

have the same number of cars? _____ and _____ Which boy has the

most, Keith or Lee? _____

How many cars does Bill have? _____

② **Write the ratio.**

The number of stars to the number of hearts   ___:___

The number of diamonds to the number of stars   ___:___

The number of hearts to the number of diamonds   ___:___

The number of hearts and stars to the number of diamonds   ___:___

The number of stars to the number of hearts and diamonds   ___:___

The number of hearts and stars to the number of stars and diamonds   ___:___

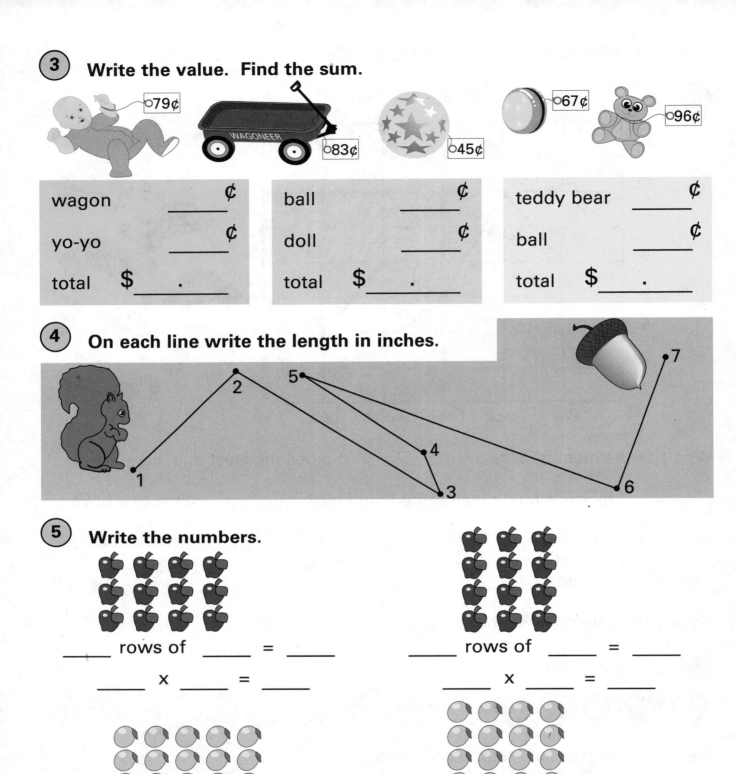

3 Write the value. Find the sum.

79¢   83¢   45¢   67¢   96¢

wagon _____ ¢	
yo-yo _____ ¢	
total $_____ . _____	

ball _____ ¢	
doll _____ ¢	
total $_____ . _____	

teddy bear _____ ¢	
ball _____ ¢	
total $_____ . _____	

4 On each line write the length in inches.

5 Write the numbers.

_____ rows of _____ = _____

_____ x _____ = _____

_____ rows of _____ = _____

_____ x _____ = _____

_____ rows of _____ = _____

_____ x _____ = _____

_____ rows of _____ = _____

_____ x _____ = _____

6 Mother ironed 5 shirts. Each shirt had 4 buttons on it.
How many buttons were on the 5 shirts?

84

1 **Solve the equations.**

n + 3 = 6	n + 8 = 12	n + 2 = 8	n + 6 = 13
n + 4 = 4	n + 5 = 9	n + 8 = 15	n + 9 = 10

2

Girls' Ages

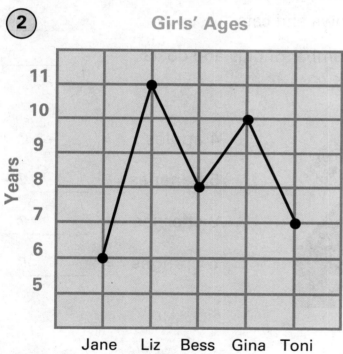

Who is the oldest? _____

Who is the youngest? _____

Toni is how much younger

than Gina? _____

Who is oldest, Bess or Jane?

_____

Bess is how much older

than Jane? _____

There are how many years

between Liz and Gina? _____

3 **Match the multiplication pairs.**

3 x 4 = 12	7 x 4 = 28
4 x 7 = 28	4 x 8 = 32
8 x 4 = 32	5 x 4 = 20
4 x 5 = 20	4 x 3 = 12

2 x 4 = 8	4 x 1 = 4
4 x 9 = 36	4 x 6 = 24
1 x 4 = 4	4 x 2 = 8
6 x 4 = 24	9 x 4 = 36

85

4 Write the ratio using the picture below.

The number of cats to the number of pigs   ____ : ____

The number of goats and cows to the number of horses   ____ : ____

The number of pigs and cats to the number of horses   ____ : ____

The number of goats to the number of cows and cats   ____ : ____

The number of cows and horses to the number of pigs and goats ____ : ____

5 Write the cost.

Cherries 3¢ each   Bananas 8¢ each   Oranges 5¢ each   Apples 7¢ each

4 apples   = _____ ¢

5 bananas = _____ ¢

9 cherries = _____ ¢

6 oranges = _____ ¢

6 Write < or >.

1 **Match the solid to its name.** **5 pts.**

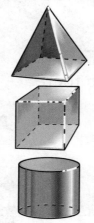

cone

cube

cylinder

pyramid

sphere

2 **Write the answers.** **6 pts.**

Is 16 closer to 10 or 20? _____

Is 38 closer to 30 or 40? _____

Is 52 closer to 50 or 60? _____

Is 49 closer to 40 or 50? _____

Is 66 closer to 60 or 70? _____

Is 72 closer to 70 or 80? _____

3 **Solve the equations.** **8 pts.**

$5 + n = 11$	$3 + n = 12$	$7 + n = 16$	$8 + n = 14$
$3 + n = 8$	$6 + n = 15$	$4 + n = 7$	$8 + n = 17$

4 **Write = or ≠.** **6 pts.**

5×9 ____ 45 2×4 ____ 8 7×5 ____ 70

3×6 ____ 24 8×3 ____ 32 6×9 ____ 36

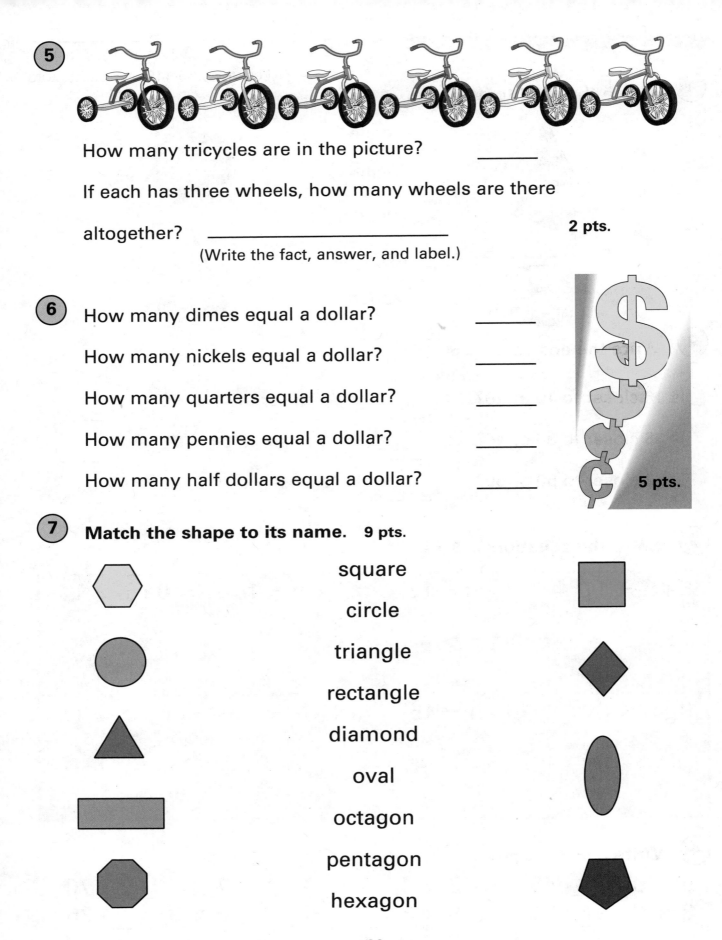

5

How many tricycles are in the picture? _____

If each has three wheels, how many wheels are there

altogether? _____   **2 pts.**
(Write the fact, answer, and label.)

6 How many dimes equal a dollar? _____

How many nickels equal a dollar? _____

How many quarters equal a dollar? _____

How many pennies equal a dollar? _____

How many half dollars equal a dollar? _____   **5 pts.**

7 **Match the shape to its name.**   **9 pts.**

square

circle

triangle

rectangle

diamond

oval

octagon

pentagon

hexagon

① Measure the objects in centimeters. Label the answers.

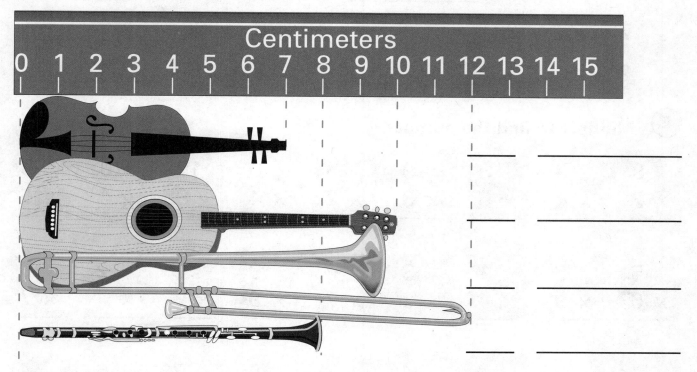

_____ _____

_____

_____

_____

② Write the value. Find the sum.

$1.69 $ 0.72 $2.02 $ 0.75

milk	$_____._____		bread	$_____._____		milk	$_____._____
grapes	$_____._____		butter	$_____._____		bread	$_____._____
total	$_____._____		total	$_____._____		total	$_____._____

③ Solve the equations.

| $n+1 = 9$ | $n + 3 = 12$ | $n + 4 = 10$ | $n + 7 = 15$ |

4 Write the multiplication fact to make a pair.

5 x 6 = 30 _____   3 x 9 = 27 _____

7 x 4 = 28 _____   10 x 6 = 60 _____

2 x 8 = 16 _____   1 x 8 = 8 _____

5 Multiply to find the product.

9 x 2	3 x 4	3 x 6	9 x 3	3 x 2	0 x 4	10 x 9	10 x 4	9 x 5

5 x 6	6 x 9	1 x 4	3 x 5	4 x 7	9 x 9	3 x 3	2 x 4	6 x 7

4 x 4	9 x 4	7 x 3	4 x 8	3 x 8	4 x 5	7 x 9	6 x 8	4 x 9

6 Write < or >.

8 + 5 ____ 13 - 4   6 + 6 ____ 7 - 3   10 - 5 ____ 9 + 7

12 - 6 ____ 5 + 9   5 - 3 ____ 1 + 2   5 + 5 ____ 9 - 6

7 Write an addition or subtraction fact.

7
4 △ 5

_____ = 12
_____ = 3
_____ = 9
_____ = 2

9
6 △ 2

_____ = 4
_____ = 11
_____ = 15
_____ = 7

8
1 △ 3

_____ = 9
_____ = 5
_____ = 11
_____ = 2

1 Write the fractional part that is colored.

2 Measure the objects in centimeters. Label the answers.

Centimeters
0 1 2 3 4 5 6 7 8 9 10 11 12 13 14 15

_____ _____

_____ _____

_____ _____

_____ _____

3 Write the answers.

Is 186 closer to 180 or 190?

Is 127 closer to 120 or 130?

Is 342 closer to 340 or 350?

Is 378 closer to 370 or 380?

Is 604 closer to 600 or 610?

Bea	👧 👧 👦 👦 👦
Cal	👦
Dennis	👧 👧 👧 👦 👦 👦
Fay	👧 👧 👧 👧
Hal	👧 👦 👦 👦 👦

Boy

Girl

Who had the most children in their family? _____

Who had the most girls in their family? _____

Who had the most boys in their family? _____

Who had the least children in their family? _____

Who had the least boys in their family? _____

Who had the least girls in their family? _____

Who had more boys than Dennis? _____

Who had fewer girls than Bea? _____

⑤ **Multiply to find the product.**

6	7	3	6	8	9	3	4	6
$\times\ 6$	$\times\ 4$	$\times\ 7$	$\times\ 5$	$\times\ 4$	$\times\ 7$	$\times\ 5$	$\times\ 3$	$\times\ 3$

6	8	4	9	7	9	3	9	2
$\times\ 9$	$\times\ 6$	$\times\ 4$	$\times\ 8$	$\times\ 6$	$\times\ 4$	$\times\ 8$	$\times\ 9$	$\times\ 7$

⑥ **Solve the equations.**

$n + 5 = 5$ $n + 2 = 10$ $n + 2 = 7$ $n + 5 = 12$

1 **Write the Roman numerals.**

I	IV	V	IX	X	XL	L	XC	C	CD	D	CM	M
1	4	5	9	10	40	50	90	100	400	500	900	1,000

138 _____

162 _____

214 _____

397 _____

550 _____

673 _____

746 _____

881 _____

2 **Write the fractional part that is colored.**

3 **Write the numbers.**

Is 386 closer to 380 or 390? _____   Is 529 closer to 520 or 530? _____

Is 754 closer to 750 or 760? _____   Is 273 closer to 270 or 280? _____

4 **Measure each object in centimeters.**

93

5 Write the multiplication fact to represent how many cans each person collected.

Tom							each
Rita							
Hanna							(any color)
Odell							equals 5
Kim							
Bev							

Tom _____   Hanna _____   Kim _____

Rita _____   Odell _____   Bev _____

Who collected the most cans? _____

How many cans did Tom and Kim collect together? _____

6 Multiply to find the product.

9	4	1	9	3	6	3	9	6
x 8	x 4	x 4	x 4	x 3	x 5	x 4	x 5	x 3

8	1	6	6	8	3	5	9	2
x 6	x 9	x 6	x 4	x 3	x 9	x 3	x 9	x 4

7 Write an addition fact or a subtraction fact.

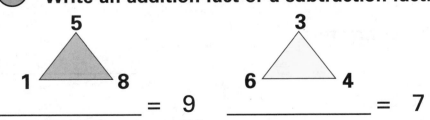

_____ = 9   _____ = 7   _____ = 5

_____ = 3   _____ = 2   _____ = 16

_____ = 7   _____ = 9   _____ = 7

_____ = 13   _____ = 3   _____ = 11

94

1   **Find the sum.**

| 3,621 +3,119 | 3,971 +1,505 | 1,958 +4,022 | 2,437 +5,661 | 8,239 +1,458 | 2,661 +3,292 |

| 5,473 +1,332 | 1,754 +3,741 | 1,243 +1,629 | 2,198 +7,640 | 7,314 +2,439 | 5,416 +3,873 |

$$n - 5 = 7$$
$$+ 5 + 5$$
$$n \qquad = 12$$

$$n - 8 = 3$$
$$+ 8 + 8$$
$$n \qquad = 11$$

$$n - 7 = 6$$
$$+ 7 + 7$$
$$n \qquad = 13$$

2   **Solve the equations.**

n - 8 = 8	n - 5 = 9	n - 0 = 2	n - 4 = 9
n - 8 = 5	n - 4 = 2	n - 6 = 8	n - 3 = 5

3   **Measure the lines in centimeters.**

4 Write the Arabic numbers.

I	IV	V	IX	X	XL	L	XC	C	CD	D	CM	M
1	4	5	9	10	40	50	90	100	400	500	900	1,000

CLVI = _____ DCCXCII = _____

DCXLIII = _____ CCCXVIII = _____

DCCCXXV = _____ DIX = _____

CDXXXVII = _____ CMLXI = _____

CCLXXX = _____ CCLXXIV = _____

5 Shade the objects for each fractional part.

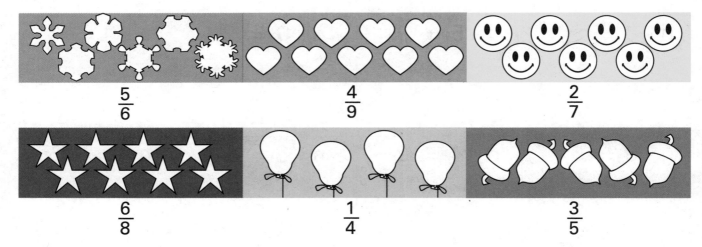

$\frac{5}{6}$ $\frac{4}{9}$ $\frac{2}{7}$

$\frac{6}{8}$ $\frac{1}{4}$ $\frac{3}{5}$

6 Multiply to find the product.

4	3	4	6	9	4	6	10	4
x 7	x 6	x 1	x 4	x 3	x 4	x 7	x 4	x 9

7
There were 123 pages in the first book Nell read. Her second book had 88 pages. How many pages did she read in both books?

1 **Write the correct time.**

:_____   :_____   :_____   :_____

:_____   :_____   :_____   :_____

2 **Find the sum.**

| 3,402 +2,468 | 7,841 +1,848 | 5,312 +2,945 | 4,072 +5,883 | 4,230 +1,683 | 4,639 +3,239 |

3 **Solve the equations.**

| $n - 1 = 3$ $+ 1 + 1$ $n =$ | $n - 5 = 9$ | $n - 0 = 2$ | $n - 4 = 9$ |

4 Fran's teacher asked her to read 150 pages in nine weeks. She has read 129 pages. How many more pages must she read before the end of the nine weeks?

(5) Shade the objects for each fractional part.

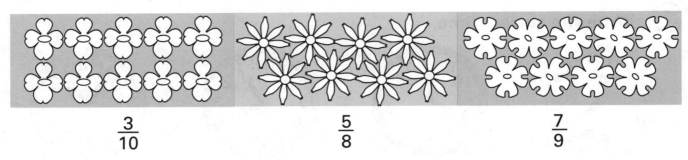

$\dfrac{3}{10}$ $\dfrac{5}{8}$ $\dfrac{7}{9}$

(6) Multiply to find the product.

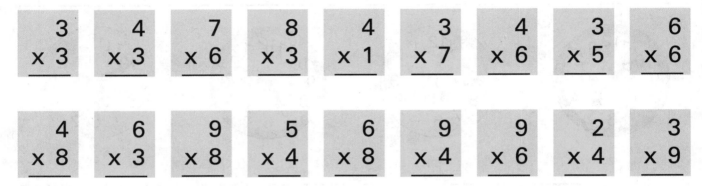

3	4	7	8	4	3	4	3	6
x 3	x 3	x 6	x 3	x 1	x 7	x 6	x 5	x 6

4	6	9	5	6	9	9	2	3
x 8	x 3	x 8	x 4	x 8	x 4	x 6	x 4	x 9

(7) Write as a number sentence.

Seventeen plus six equals twenty-three.   _____

Twenty-five increased by seven is thirty-two.   _____

Twelve minus eight equals four.   _____

Sixty added to forty is one hundred.   _____

(8) Match the shapes.

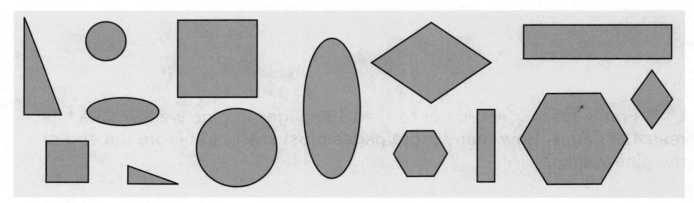

1 **Write the numbers.**

circle sets of 2's

_____ sets of 2's

$\frac{1}{2}$ of 8 = _____

circle sets of 3's

_____ sets of 3's

$\frac{1}{3}$ of 12 = _____

circle sets of 5's

_____ sets of 5's

$\frac{1}{5}$ of 10 = _____

circle sets of 2's

_____ sets of 2's

$\frac{1}{2}$ of 14 = _____

circle sets of 3's

_____ sets of 3's

$\frac{1}{3}$ of 15 = _____

circle sets of 4's

_____ sets of 4's

$\frac{1}{4}$ of 16 = _____

2 **Solve the equations.**

n - 5 = 7	n - 1 = 4	n - 9 = 9	n - 9 = 0

3 **Multiply to find the product.**

3 x 6	7 x 6	9 x 6	1 x 6	6 x 4	6 x 8	6 x 2	6 x 6	6 x 0

4 x 3	4 x 6	8 x 9	4 x 9	5 x 4	9 x 9	4 x 7	7 x 9	4 x 4

4 Draw both hands on the clocks.

         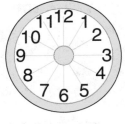

5:20   8:50   3:05   11:30

5 Find the sum.

| 5,089 +4,312 | 1,363 +6,576 | 2,590 +4,167 | 6,822 +1,402 | 4,257 +2,705 | 5,514 +3,925 |

6 Match the shape to its name.

diamond
square
rectangle
circle
oval
triangle
hexagon
pentagon
octagon

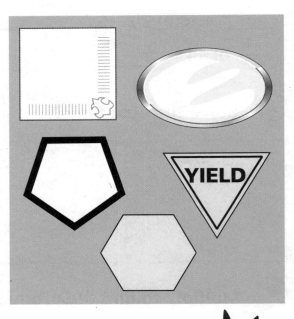

7 Write a word problem about the picture.

_____

_____

_____

100

16 ounces (oz.) = 1 pound (lb.)

2,000 pounds (lbs.) = 1 Ton (T.)

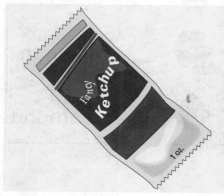

1 Ton

(1) **Match the picture to the estimated weight.**

1 ton

1 pound

180 pounds

16 pounds

60 pounds

1 ounce

(2) **Find the sum.**

6,021	3,715	1,632	3,160	3,412	2,835
+3,139	+3,237	+7,281	+4,585	+4,806	+2,712

(3) **Find the difference and check.**

290	714	624	846	912	783	519
- 253	- 650	- 594	- 291	- 103	- 265	- 379

④ Write = or ≠.

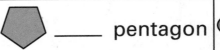 _____ triangle   _____ pentagon   _____ circle

_____ rectangle   _____ oval   _____ octagon

_____ hexagon   _____ square   _____ diamond

⑤ Write the numbers.

1 year = _____ months	1 week = _____ days
1 hour = _____ minutes	1 minute = _____ seconds
1 day = _____ hours	$\frac{1}{2}$ hour = _____ minutes
1 year = _____ weeks	1 year = _____ days

⑥ Write the numbers.

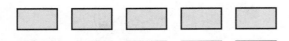      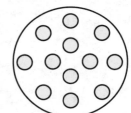

circle sets of 2's   circle sets of 3's   circle sets of 4's

_____ sets of 2's   _____ sets of 3's   _____ sets of 4's

$\frac{1}{2}$ of 10 = _____ $\frac{1}{3}$ of 9 = _____ $\frac{1}{4}$ of 12 = _____

⑦ Write the numbers.

three 7's = ___ + ___ + ___ = ___ x ___ = ___

seven 7's = ___ + ___ + ___ + ___ + ___ + ___ + ___ = ___ x ___ = ___

four 7's = ___ + ___ + ___ + ___ = ___ x ___ = ___

Draw the nickels needed on the pictograph.

Nickels Spent at Lunch

each

equals 5¢

Chris	
Ray	
Ben	
George	
Kent	
Larry	
Mel	

Chris   – 25¢

Ray   – 40¢

Ben   – 45¢

George – 30¢

Kent   – 20¢

Larry   – 35¢

Mel   – 30¢

2 Write <, >, or =.

 Match the pairs of multiplication facts.

7 x 2 = 14 7 x 4 = 28	10 x 7 = 70 7 x 10 = 70
4 x 7 = 28 2 x 7 = 14	1 x 7 = 7 7 x 1 = 7

4 Write the numbers.

1 minute = _____ seconds

1 year = _____ months

1 week = _____ days

1 hour = _____ minutes

103

5 Match the solid to its picture.

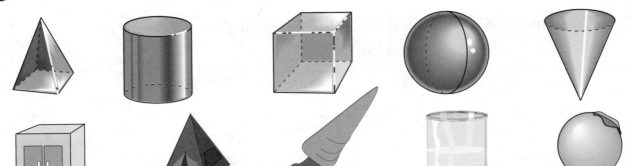

6 Write the numbers.

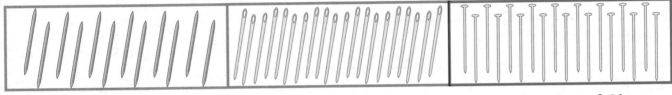

circle sets of 2's

_____ sets of 2's

$\frac{1}{2}$ of 12 = _____

circle sets of 4's

_____ sets of 4's

$\frac{1}{4}$ of 20 = _____

circle sets of 3's

_____ sets of 3's

$\frac{1}{3}$ of 18 = _____

7 Solve the equations.

$n + 6 = 13$	$4 + n = 12$	$6 + n = 8$	$n + 3 = 6$

8 Write the next three numbers in the series.

4	1	4	1	4	1	_____	_____	_____
3	5	2	3	5	2	_____	_____	_____
7	6	0	9	7	6	_____	_____	_____
8	1	5	8	1	5	_____	_____	_____

1 **Write ones', tens', hundreds', or thousands'.**

2,483 has an 8 in the _____ place.

2,483 has a 2 in the _____ place.

9,048 has an 8 in the _____ place.

9,048 has a 0 in the _____ place.

5,617 has a 5 in the _____ place.

5,617 has a 7 in the _____ place.

3,564 has a 6 in the _____ place.

3,564 has a 5 in the _____ place.

2 **Write the next three numbers in the series.**

1	2	5	3	1	2			
4	7	6	8	4	7			
9	3	0	2	9	3			
5	4	1	7	5	4			

3 **Write the name of the solid.**

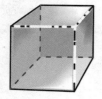    

_____ _____ _____ _____

4 Josh's mother bought 4 bags of apples. There were 9 apples in each bag. How many apples did Josh's mother buy?

⑤ Solve the equations.

0 + n = 4	4 + n = 9	n + 8 = 15	n + 9 = 10

⑥ Write the number of points each boy scored.

Touchdowns in a Year

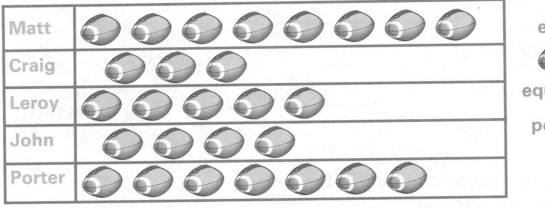

each

equals 6

points

Leroy _____   John _____   Porter _____   Matt _____   Craig _____

⑦ Find the product.

4	7	9	4	10	7	4	3	9
x 0	x 8	x 5	x 1	x 4	x 5	x 2	x 7	x 3

9	4	4	6	10	7	9	7	6
x 9	x 5	x 7	x 3	x 9	x 7	x 8	x 4	x 4

⑧ Find the difference.

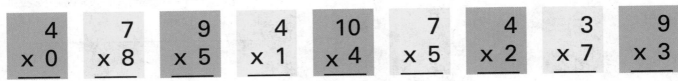

877	582	639	405	367	291	685
- 808	- 147	- 377	- 265	- 284	- 38	- 208

(1) Measure the lines in inches.

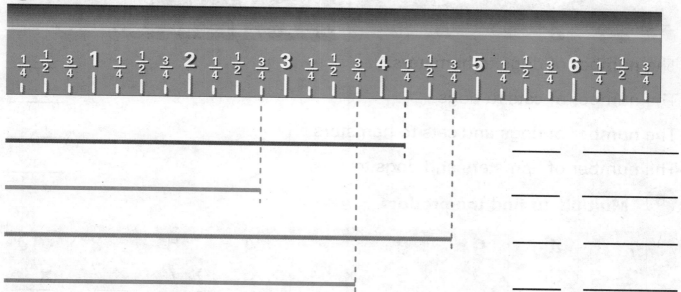

_____   _____

_____   _____

_____   _____

_____   _____

(2) Find the sum.

2,902	7,579	1,068	4,744	1,569	1,839
+1,829	+2,333	+5,859	+1,663	+2,507	+6,224

(3) Write ones', tens', hundreds', or thousands'.

3,956 has a 5 in the _____ place.

3,956 has a 3 in the _____ place.

3,956 has a 6 in the _____ place.

3,956 has a 9 in the _____ place.

(4) Find the difference.

590	737	472	653	181	942	845
- 468	- 387	- 313	- 471	- 154	- 217	- 392

5 Write the ratio using the picture below.

The number of dogs to hamsters. ___ : ___

The number of cats to dogs. ___ : ___

The number of dogs and cats to hamsters. ___ : ___

The number of hamsters and dogs to cats. ___ : ___

6 Multiply to find the product.

7	4	9	3	7	4	8	3	10
x 2	x 3	x 9	x 9	x 5	x 8	x 7	x 7	x 5

9	4	8	7	4	9	6	4	7
x 4	x 7	x 9	x 7	x 5	x 6	x 7	x 4	x 4

7 Solve the equations.

n + 5 = 13	6 + n = 12	9 + n = 16	n + 3 = 10

8 Jacob found 5 bird nests. Each nest had 3 eggs. How many eggs did Jacob find in all?

Mother bought 8 yards of cloth for $4.00 a yard. How much did she spend?

(1)

Temperature Highs

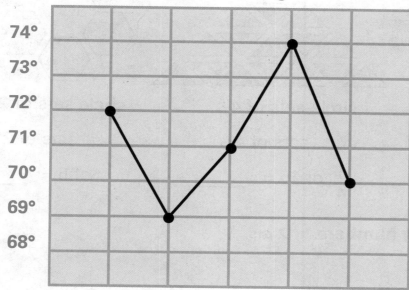

4 pts.

Mon. Tues. Wed. Thurs.   Fri.

What day had the highest temperature? _____

Tuesday was how much colder than Monday? _____

What was the temperature on Wednesday? _____

Wednesday was how much warmer than Friday? _____

(2) Find the sum. 6 pts.

| 4,102 +3,148 | 5,361 +4,164 | 3,034 +5,694 | 1,754 +7,710 | 7,472 +1,904 | 4,625 +2,138 |

(3) Solve the equations. 4 pts.

| $n - 3 = 10$ | $n - 8 = 7$ | $n - 5 = 11$ | $n - 5 = 9$ |

4 Write the numbers. 6 pts.

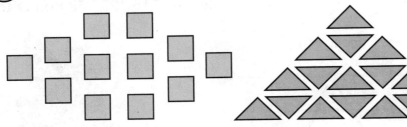

circle sets of 3's

_____ sets of 3's

$\frac{1}{3}$ of 12 = _____

circle sets of 4's

_____ sets of 4's

$\frac{1}{4}$ of 16 = _____

circle sets of 2's

_____ sets of 2's

$\frac{1}{2}$ of 6 = _____

5 Write the next three numbers. 12 pts.

5	4	8	5	4			
2	3	2	3	2	___	___	___
1	0	4	1	0	___	___	___
7	9	7	9	7	___	___	___

6 Multiply to find the product. 9 pts.

10	0	10	7	2	7	1	5	9
x 3	x 9	x 7	x 0	x 8	x 5	x 9	x 5	x 2

7 Find the difference. 7 pts.

678	624	923	938	709	365	581
- 659	- 317	- 483	- 457	- 598	- 290	- 425

8 Neil gathered 32 hickory nuts in the woods. Perry gathered 59 walnuts. How many nuts did the boys gather altogether?

1 pt.

Sunday	–	Sun.			
Monday	–	Mon.	Thursday	–	Thurs.
Tuesday	–	Tues.	Friday	–	Fri.
Wednesday	–	Wed.	Saturday	–	Sat.

① Write the shortened form for the days of the week.

third day _____   second day _____   first day _____

fifth day _____   sixth day _____   fourth day _____

seventh day _____

② Find the difference.

215 - 185	894 - 76	927 - 560	840 - 321	853 - 419	758 - 498	696 - 437

③ Write the correct letter in the blank.

G	P	I	N
543	362	604	710

R	S	T
827	469	975

276 +328   583 +392   307 +297   180 +289

_____ _____   _____ _____

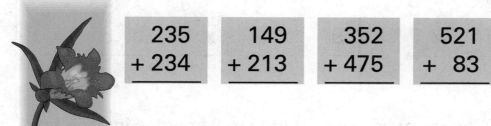

235 + 234   149 + 213   352 + 475   521 + 83   526 +184   276 +267

_____   _____

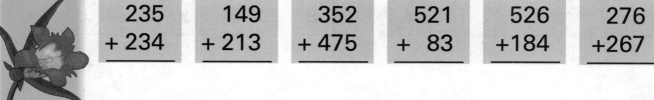

111

4 **Measure the lines in inches.**

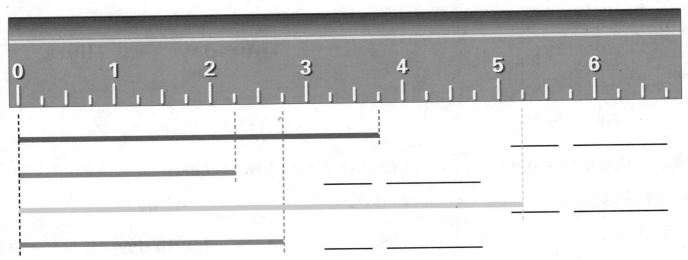

5 **Write the ratio using the picture below.**

The number of tops and drums to the number of teddy bears ___ : ___

The number of tops and drums to the number of teddy bears and drums ___ : ___

The number of teddy bears and tops to the number of drums and tops ___ : ___

6 **Multiply to find the product.**

5	4	10	3	7	9	9	0	7
x 7	x 9	x 7	x 4	x 4	x 6	x 7	x 4	x 2

4	3	4	8	5	3	7	8	4
x 2	x 7	x 1	x 7	x 9	x 9	x 6	x 6	x 8

7 The teacher had 4 boxes of crayons. There are 8 crayons in each box. How many crayons does the teacher have?

1 **Find the sum.**

$ 4.83 + $ 2.75 = $4.83
+2.75

$ 6.28 + $ 0.64 = $6.28
+0.64

$32.15 + $21.85 =

+_____

$68.94 + $ 0.76 =

+_____

$12.97 + $ 5.60 =

+_____

$84.80 + $12.31 =

+_____

2 **Measure the lines in inches.**

____ _____

____ _____

____ _____

____ _____

3 At the basketball game there were 5 rows of bleachers. If 9 students could sit in each row, how many students could sit on the bleachers?

④ Solve the equations.

n - 7 = 9	n - 5 = 5	n - 2 = 0	n - 9 = 3

⑤ Count the squares to find the area. We measure area in square units.

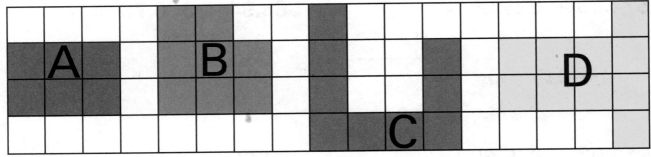

The area of A is _____ square centimeters.

The area of B is _____ square centimeters.

The area of C is _____ square centimeters.

The area of D is _____ square centimeters.

⑥ Find the difference.

682	507	977	914	693	671	929
- 569	- 343	- 887	- 631	- 124	- 262	- 140

⑦ Multiply to find the product.

3	6	9	4	1	4	5	4	0
x 4	x 4	x 8	x 7	x 4	x 9	x 6	x 2	x 3

114

① Find the difference.

$33.28 - $31.31 = - _____	$65.04 - $32.74 = - _____
$27.80 - $ 1.51 = - _____	$74.73 - $ 3.28 = - _____
$45.18 - $ 0.97 = - _____	$51.56 - $ 0.76 = - _____

② Count the squares to find the area.

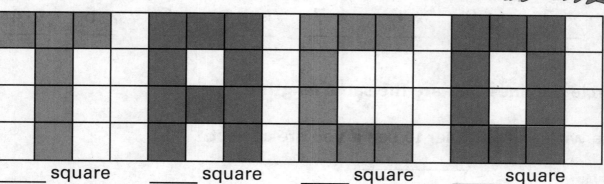

_____ square centimeters   _____ square centimeters   _____ square centimeters   _____ square centimeters

③ Find the sum.

1,579	5,787	3,863	4,856	2,948	3,978
+1,645	+3,749	+2,297	+1,684	+4,173	+1,465

④ Write the length in inches on each line.

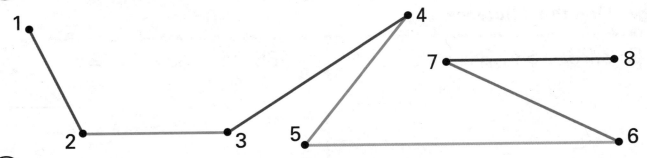

⑤ Solve the equations.

n - 9 = 4	n - 7 = 0	n - 7 = 7	n - 6 = 2

⑥ Multiply to find the product.

9	4	8	7	8	4	10	7	2
x 9	x 4	x 7	x 1	x 9	x 7	x 7	x 2	x 4

4	7	5	3	6	6	7	9	10
x 6	x 3	x 6	x 4	x 7	x 3	x 5	x 5	x 4

⑦ Circle the lines that are the same length as line AB.

A _____ B

Measure with an inch ruler to see if you are correct.

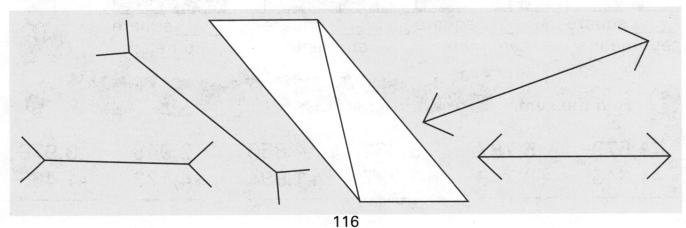

116

1 **Measure the line to the nearest inch.**

_____ _____

_____ _____

_____ _____

_____ _____

2   **2nd Grade Classroom**

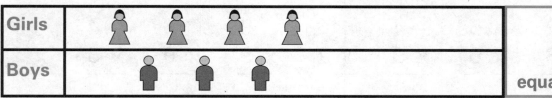 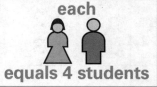

How many girls are in the class? _____ How many boys are in the class?

_____ How many more girls are there than boys? _____

How many are in the class altogether? _____

3 **Find the difference.**

262	734	840	571	881	901	736
- 225	- 416	- 516	- 490	- 172	- 431	- 195

4 **Find the sum.**

2,317	2,714	1,247	4,567	4,958	3,689
+3,729	+6,659	+8,263	+2,740	+4,714	+4,271

5 Shade the number of squares needed to equal the
following areas:

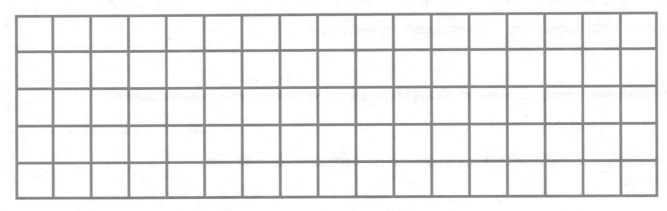

| 8 square centimeters | 11 square centimeters | 7 square centimeters | 5 square centimeters |

6 Multiply to find the product.

| 6 | 2 | 5 | 4 | 6 | 9 | 6 | 4 | 7 |
| x 6 | x 3 | x 6 | x 9 | x 7 | x 9 | x 0 | x 3 | x 2 |

7 Solve the equations.

| n - 6 = 7 | n - 7 = 8 | n - 1 = 8 | n - 9 = 2 |

8 Write an addition fact or a subtraction fact.

7
3 △ 5

4
1 △ 9

6
2 △ 8

_____ = 8   _____ = 8   _____ = 8

_____ = 10   _____ = 5   _____ = 6

_____ = 4   _____ = 13   _____ = 14

_____ = 12   _____ = 10   _____ = 4

118

① **Write the numbers.**

circle sets of 4's   circle sets of 3's   circle sets of 5's

shade 3 in each set   shade 2 in each set   shade 4 in each set

$\frac{3}{4}$ of 8 = _____ $\frac{2}{3}$ of 12 = _____ $\frac{4}{5}$ of 15 = _____

② **Write the numbers.**

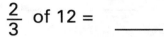

1 pound (lb.) = [____] ounces (oz.)   1 ton (T.) = [____] pounds (lbs.)

Write < or >.

5 lbs. flour _____ 5 ounces flour   8 ounces juice _____ 8 T. juice

3 tons coal _____ 3 pounds coal   25 lbs. sugar _____ 22 T. sugar

4 oz. milk _____ 3 pounds milk   17 T. candy _____ 17 oz. candy

③   **Blocks from School**

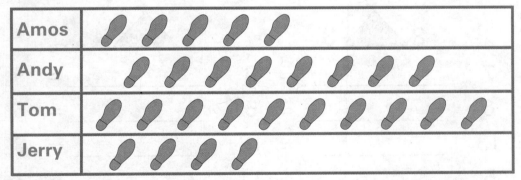

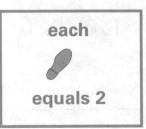

How many blocks did each boy live from school?

Amos _____   **Andy** _____   **Tom** _____   **Jerry** _____

Who lived the closest? _____ Jerry lived how much closer than Tom?

_____ Amos lived how much closer than Andy? _____

119

4 **Measure the lines to the nearest inch.**

_____ _____

_____ _____

_____ _____

_____ _____

5 **Find the product.**

10 x 9	9 x 5	5 x 7	7 x 4	2 x 9	6 x 9	7 x 6	9 x 3	7 x 2

8 x 7	1 x 9	8 x 9	3 x 7	9 x 4	7 x 7	9 x 7	9 x 9	0 x 9

6 **Write an addition fact or a subtraction fact.**

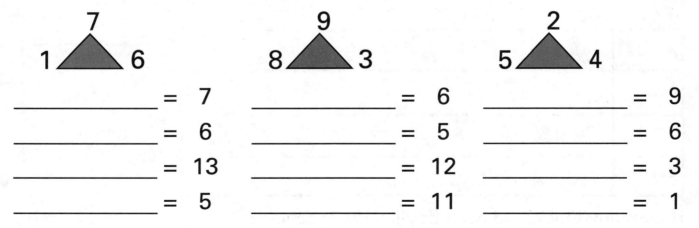

7
1 △ 6

_____ = 7
_____ = 6
_____ = 13
_____ = 5

9
8 △ 3

_____ = 6
_____ = 5
_____ = 12
_____ = 11

2
5 △ 4

_____ = 9
_____ = 6
_____ = 3
_____ = 1

7 Andrea threw her paper route in 48 minutes on Monday. On Tuesday she decreased her time by 12 minutes. How long did it take her to throw her paper route on Tuesday?

1 **Write the numbers.**

1 hour = _____ minutes	1 year = _____ weeks
1 day = _____ hours	1 minute = _____ seconds
1 year = _____ days	1 week = _____ days
$\frac{1}{2}$ hour = _____ minutes	1 year = _____ months

2 **Write the numbers.**

circle sets of 5's

shade 2 in each set

$\frac{2}{5}$ of 10 = _____

circle sets of 3's

shade 2 in each set

$\frac{2}{3}$ of 15 = _____

circle sets of 4's

shade 2 in each set

$\frac{2}{4}$ of 12 = _____

3 **Write two word problems about the pictures and solve them.**

$ 0.35 $2.53 $ 0.87 $ 0.56

_____   _____

_____   _____

_____   _____

_____   _____

_____   _____

4 Find the perimeter.

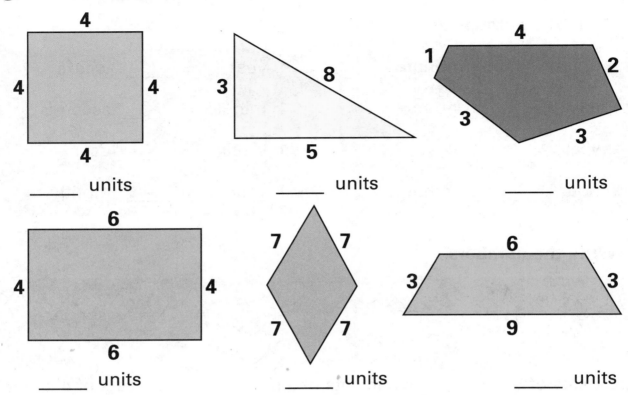

_____ units   _____ units   _____ units

_____ units   _____ units   _____ units

5 Find the sum.

8,641	3,975	5,728	2,959	4,389	1,689
+ 689	+2,286	+1,593	+2,693	+3,964	+2,995

6 Find the difference.

920	722	315	420	812	611	935
- 842	- 348	- 238	- 268	- 348	- 116	- 667

7 Find the product.

7	4	7	7	6	6	7	6	9
x 4	x 4	x 5	x 7	x 7	x 6	x 8	x 4	x 7

1 **Write the numbers.**

three 8's   = ___ + ___ + ___ = ___ x ___ = ___

four 8's   = ___ + ___ + ___ + ___ = ___ x ___ = ___

two 8's   = ___ + ___ = ___ x ___ = ___

eight 8's   = ___ + ___ + ___ + ___ + ___ + ___ + ___ + ___ = ___ x ___ = ___

five 8's   = ___ + ___ + ___ + ___ + ___ = ___ x ___ = ___

nine 8's   = ___ + ___ + ___ + ___ + ___ + ___ + ___ + ___ + ___ = ___ x ___ = ___

six 8's   = ___ + ___ + ___ + ___ + ___ + ___ = ___ x ___ = ___

seven 8's   = ___ + ___ + ___ + ___ + ___ + ___ + ___ = ___ x ___ = ___

2 **Write the numbers.**

circle sets of 3's   circle sets of 7's   circle sets of 5's

shade 2 in each set   shade 4 in each set   shade 3 in each set

$\frac{2}{3}$ of 9 = ____ $\frac{4}{7}$ of 14 = ____ $\frac{3}{5}$ of 10 = ____

3 **Write as a number sentence.**

Fifty-six and forty equals ninety-six.   _____

Seventy-one less thirty-six is thirty-five.   _____

Fifteen subtracted from thirty-eight is twenty-three.   _____

Forty-three more than twenty equals sixty-three.   _____

Seven take away five equals two.   _____

4 Find the difference.

| 512
- 346 | 713
- 594 | 840
- 475 | 734
- 285 | 646
- 387 | 450
- 379 | 965
- 396 |

5 Find the perimeter.

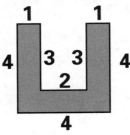

_____ units

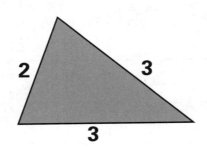

_____ units

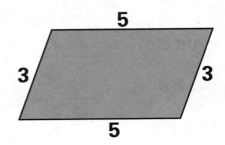

_____ units

6 Find the sum.

| 5,128
+4,496 | 3,460
+5,865 | 4,157
+4,268 | 2,796
+1,470 | 7,295
+2,418 | 1,362
+7,997 |

7 Write two word problems about the picture and solve them.

"Home of the flying burger" **Freddy's Fast Food** *Where BURGERS have wings.*

Hamburger..... 99¢ French Fries ...79¢ Milk.............50¢
Hot Dog........ 79¢ Pizza............. 69¢ Pop.............. 60¢
Chili Dog .... 89¢ Ice Cream......39¢ Milk Shake .... 90¢

_____   _____

_____   _____

_____   _____

_____   _____

_____   _____

_____   _____

124

1 **Circle the shapes that have a line of symmetry drawn.**

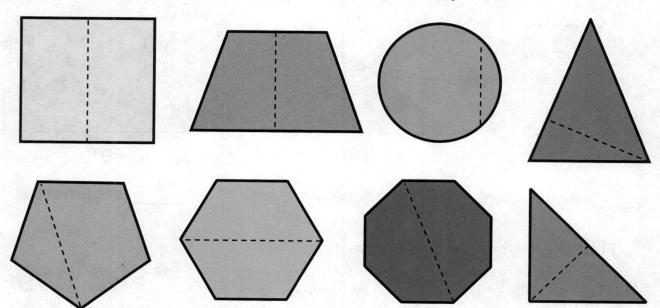

2 **Number the events in the order that they happen.**

_____ I chose a book at the library.

_____ I went to the library.

_____ I read my library book.

_____ I wore my new shoes to school.

_____ I bought a new pair of shoes.

_____ I went shopping.

3 **Write <, >, or =.**

7 x 5 ____ 42	8 x 7 ____ 49	7 x 7 ____ 56
7 x 3 ____ 14	9 x 7 ____ 56	7 x 6 ____ 49
4 x 7 ____ 28	2 x 7 ____ 14	7 x 1 ____ 7

4 Measure the sides with a centimeter ruler. Write the length by the sides. Find the perimeter.

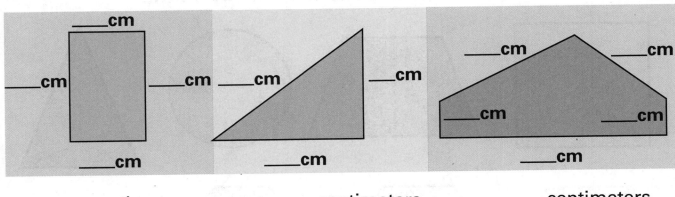

_____ centimeters   _____ centimeters   _____ centimeters

5 Find the difference and check.

918	350	931	820	834	542	750
- 539	- 191	- 248	- 654	- 276	- 179	- 487

6 Write the numbers.

1 week = _____ days	1 year = _____ weeks	
1 year = _____ days	1 day = _____ hours	
1 hour = _____ minutes	1 year = _____ months	
1 minute = _____ seconds	$\frac{1}{2}$ hour = _____ minutes	

7 Write as a number sentence.

Forty-two plus sixteen equals fifty-eight.   _____

Fifty-six decreased by twenty-three is thirty-three.   _____

Eighty-four minus seventy-two is twelve.   _____

Thirty-five plus twenty-one is fifty-six.   _____

126

① **Write the ratio.**

3 cars to 8 trucks   ___ : ___

3 cats and 2 dogs to 7 hamsters   ___ : ___

5 fingers to 5 toes   ___ : ___

2 legs to 10 toes and 10 fingers   ___ : ___

2 apples and 3 oranges to 4 pears and 5 peaches   ___ : ___

② **Circle the shapes that have a line of symmetry drawn.**

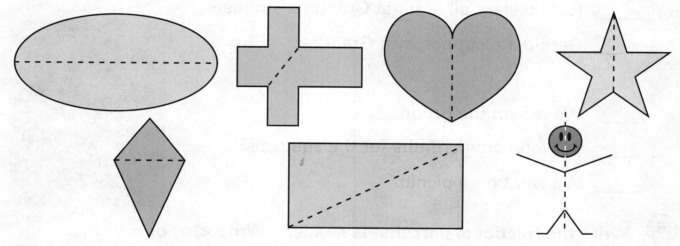

③ **Find the product.**

9 x 7	3 x 8	7 x 3	3 x 9	6 x 8	5 x 7	6 x 4	4 x 2	10 x 7
5 x 9	4 x 4	5 x 8	4 x 7	3 x 4	0 x 8	6 x 9	3 x 6	8 x 8
2 x 7	6 x 6	6 x 5	7 x 8	9 x 9	5 x 4	7 x 7	10 x 8	9 x 4

4 Find the perimeter.

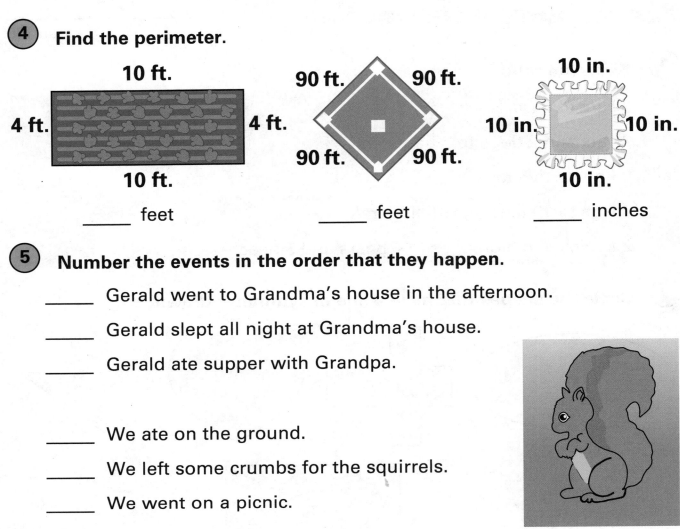

10 ft.

4 ft.   4 ft.

10 ft.

_____ feet

90 ft.   90 ft.

90 ft.   90 ft.

_____ feet

10 in.

10 in.   10 in.

10 in.

_____ inches

5 Number the events in the order that they happen.

_____ Gerald went to Grandma's house in the afternoon.

_____ Gerald slept all night at Grandma's house.

_____ Gerald ate supper with Grandpa.

_____ We ate on the ground.

_____ We left some crumbs for the squirrels.

_____ We went on a picnic.

6 Write the fractional part that is shaded. Write <, >, or = between each set of fractions.

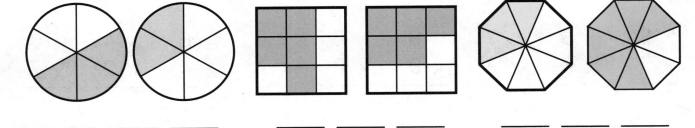

_____ _____   _____   _____ _____

7 Find the difference and check.

731	820	843	725	916	664	975
- 252	- 748	- 359	- 586	- 159	- 378	- 897

1 Circle the next picture in sequence.

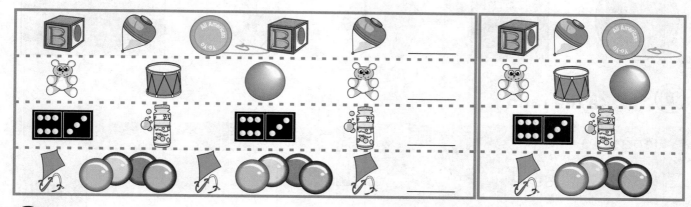

2 Match the solid to its name.

cone

cube

cylinder

pyramid

sphere

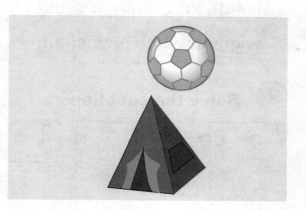

3 Write the correct time.

:   :   :   :

4 Find the sum.

3,295	1,879	3,696	4,639	4,491	3,747
+4,845	+6,362	+2,815	+2,376	+1,789	+4,469

5 **Draw a line of symmetry on each shape.**

  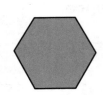  

6 **Write the ratio.**

length to width	___ : ___
width to length	___ : ___
length and width to length	___ : ___
length and width to width	___ : ___
width to width and length	___ : ___

5 width

12 length

7 **Solve the equations.**

n - 6 = 7	n - 4 = 8	n + 2 = 10	5 + n = 14

8 **Find the product.**

8	6	6	2	7	6	3	9	10
x 0	x 5	x 8	x 7	x 3	x 4	x 8	x 4	x 4

7	2	4	6	5	4	7	5	4
x 4	x 8	x 4	x 7	x 9	x 3	x 8	x 7	x 2

8	7	5				8	6	9
x 8	x 7	x 4				x 9	x 9	x 2

130

①

Stamp Collection

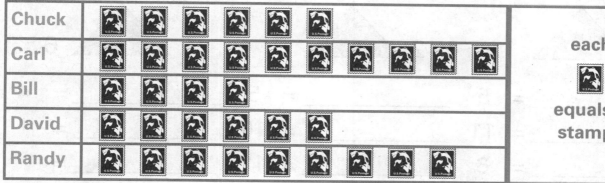

Chuck _____   Carl _____   Bill _____   David _____   Randy _____

Which boy had the most stamps? _____ What 2 boys had the same

number of stamps? _____ and _____ Which boy had the least

stamps? _____ Carl had how many more stamps than Randy? _____

Bill and David had how many stamps together? _____

11 pts.

② Write the numbers.   4 pts.

2,786 has a _____ in the tens' place.

2,786 has a _____ in the thousands' place.

2,786 has a _____ in the hundreds' place.

2,786 has a _____ in the ones' place.

③ Write the correct time.   4 pts.

___:___   ___:___   ___:___   ___:___

④ Write an addition fact or a subtraction fact. 12 pts.

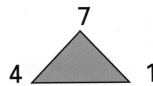
7
4   1

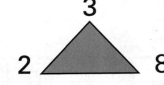
3
2   8

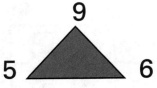
9
5   6

_____ = 5   _____ = 5   _____ = 4

_____ = 11   _____ = 10   _____ = 1

_____ = 6   _____ = 11   _____ = 11

_____ = 3   _____ = 1   _____ = 15

⑤ Write the ratio. 4 pts.

cherries to bananas   ___ : ___

apples to cherries   ___ : ___

bananas and apples to cherries   ___ : ___

apples to cherries and bananas   ___ : ___

⑥ Find the sum. 2 pts.

$16.84 + $ 2.53 = +____	$58.17 + $ 0.49 = +____

⑦ Cindy bought 7 lollipops at 8¢ each. How much money did she spend for the lollipops?   1 pt.

1 **Number the events in the order that they happen.**

_____ John bought Jack a birthday gift.

_____ John gave Jack his birthday gift.

_____ John went to Jack's birthday party.

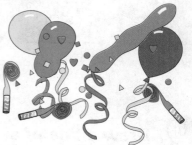

_____ Susie pulled weeds from around the young tomato plants.

_____ Susie helped Mother plant tomatoes.

_____ Susie picked tomatoes from the plants.

2 **Solve the equations.**

$n + 3 = 10$	$n - 8 = 7$	$5 + n = 14$	$n - 1 = 5$

3 **Circle the next picture in sequence.**

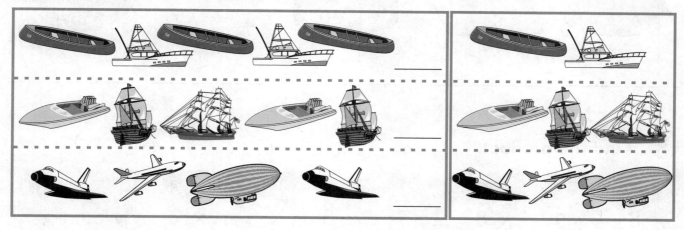

4 **Find the sum.**

7,495 +1,557	1,966 +5,358	3,479 +3,632	4,287 +3,893	6,846 +2,294	2,577 +6,954

(5) Find the difference and check.

624	930	815	562	713	480	371
- 479	- 566	- 449	- 286	- 468	- 195	- 289

(6) Draw a line of symmetry on each object.

 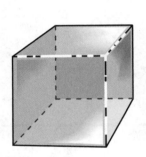  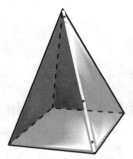

(7) Write the name of each solid.

_____ _____ _____ _____ _____

(8) Find the product.

7	3	2	3	8	4	3	3	10
x 8	x 1	x 8	x 3	x 5	x 3	x 2	x 8	x 3

5	8	8	3	8	10	6	8	3
x 3	x 4	x 8	x 7	x 0	x 8	x 3	x 1	x 9

1 **Find the difference and check.**

$$
\begin{array}{r} {}^{5}\!\!\not{6}\,{}^{9}\!\!\not{0}\,{}^{1}\!\!\not{0} \\ -\ 169 \\ \hline 431 \end{array}
\qquad
\begin{array}{r} {}^{9}\!\!\not{1}\,{}^{1}\!\!\not{0}0 \\ -\ 46 \\ \hline 54 \end{array}
$$

900	400	600	500	300
- 518	- 236	- 425	- 317	- 136

800	700	500	400	800	200	700
- 642	- 351	- 453	- 277	- 234	- 182	- 196

2 **Draw a shape equal to the area.**

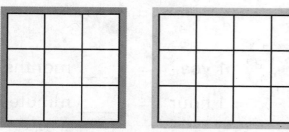

4 square
centimeters

7 square
centimeters

5 square
centimeters

10 square
centimeters

3 **Write <, >, or =.**

1 cup = 8 ounces   1 quart = 2 pints   1 gallon = 4 quarts

1 pint = 2 cups   1 quart = 4 cups

1 cup _____ 1 pint	1 quart _____ 1 pint	1 gallon _____ 1 pint
1 ounce _____ 1 cup	1 quart _____ 1 gallon	1 pint _____ 2 cups

4 Animal Heights

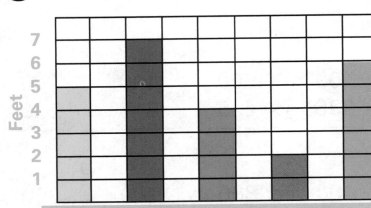

Which animal is about 4 feet tall? _____ Which animal is the shortest? _____

How tall is the bear? _____

Which animal is the tallest? _____

How tall is the horse? _____

5 Match the clock.

11:20

9:10

4:55

2:30

1 year = _____ months

1 hour = _____ minutes

1 week = _____ days

1 day = _____ hours

1 year = _____ days

6 Solve the equations.

n + 7 = 15	4 + n = 12	n - 6 = 6	n - 3 = 6

7 Ann had 4 boxes of pencils with 8 pencils in each box. How many pencils did Ann have altogether?

1 **Write the temperature.**

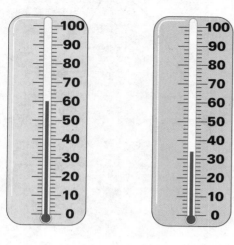 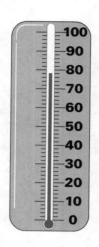  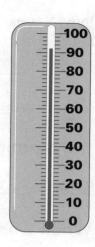

_____   _____   _____   _____   _____

2 **Write <, >, or =.**

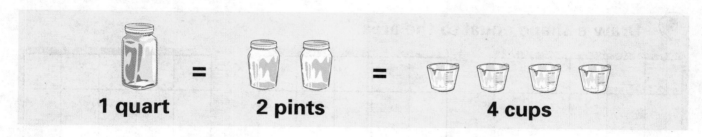

1 quart = **2 pints** = **4 cups**

1 quart _____ 4 cups	4 cups _____ 3 pints	1 pint _____ 1 cup
2 pints _____ 3 cups	2 pints _____ 1 quart	1 pint _____ 2 cups

3 **Draw the lines using an inch ruler.**

$3\frac{1}{2}$ inch •

$5\frac{1}{4}$ inch •

$4\frac{3}{4}$ inch •

(4)

When was it the hottest? _____

What was the temperature at

noon? _____

When was it coldest, 6:00 in

the morning or 6:00 in the

afternoon? _____

When was it 66°? _____

What was the temperature at 6:00 in

the afternoon? _____

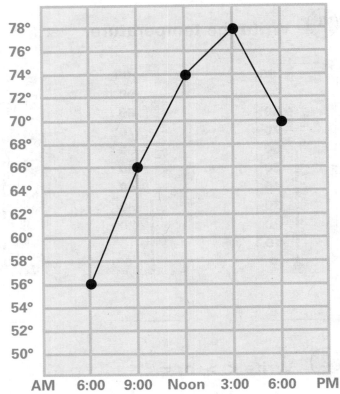

Hourly Temperatures

(5) Draw a shape equal to the area.

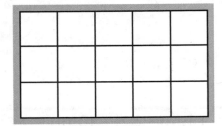

9 square centimeters

6 square centimeters

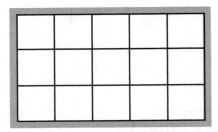

12 square centimeters

(6) Find the difference and check.

400 - 119	600 - 387	700 - 361	100 - 42	900 - 686	300 - 135	600 - 257

500 - 398	800 - 513	200 - 147	400 - 293	700 - 426	500 - 252	800 - 341

1 Fill in the blanks.

Number Correct on Speed Drill

Karen	☺☺☺☺☺☺☺
Patti	☺☺☺☺☺☺☺
Jimmer	☺☺☺☺☺☺☺☺
Jayne	☺☺☺☺☺
Tom	☺☺☺☺☺☺

each ☺ equals 2 correct

Who had the most correct?

_____ How many? _____

Who needs additional drill the

most? _____ Who had the

same number correct?

_____ and _____ How many? _____   Who had 12 correct? _____

2 Circle the correct answer.

Coffee is drunk by the _____ .   ounce   cup   quart

Mother buys milk by the _____ .   cup   ounce   gallon

Motor oil is put in a car by the _____ .   cup   pint   quart

Medicine is taken by the _____ .   pint   gallon   ounce

1 pint = ☐ cups   1 quart = ☐ pints   1 gallon = ☐ pints

3 Find the sum.

1,322	2,104	2,232	4,013	3,514	1,422
2,360	2,811	1,785	1,981	1,890	4,854
+1,877	+1,891	+3,750	+2,974	+1,263	+1,470

4 Write <, >, or =.

1 day _____ 24 hours   1 year _____ 50 weeks

1 week _____ 5 days   1 year _____ 365 days

1 year _____ 14 months $\frac{1}{2}$ hour _____ 40 minutes

139

5) Draw the lines using an inch ruler.

$4\frac{1}{2}$ inch

$2\frac{1}{4}$ inch

$3\frac{3}{4}$ inch

6) Find the product.

8	4	8	6	4	8	10	5	4
x 8	x 2	x 4	x 9	x 7	x 2	x 8	x 8	x 4

4	1	6	6	5	9	9	8	4
x 3	x 8	x 4	x 8	x 4	x 8	x 7	x 3	x 9

7) Write the correct temperature.

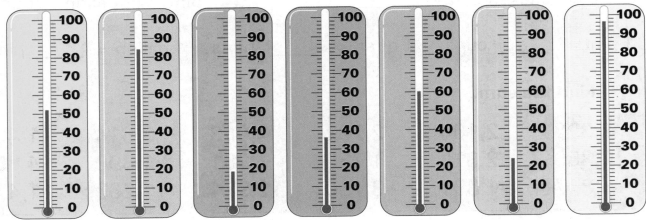

8) Find the difference.

700	500	900	300	600	800	400
- 161	- 241	- 576	- 292	- 425	- 453	- 348

① Write the Roman numerals.

I	IV	V	IX	X	XL	L	XC	C	CD	D	CM	M
1	4	5	9	10	40	50	90	100	400	500	900	1,000

183 _____   392 _____

457 _____   946 _____

824 _____   709 _____

② Measure the sides of each shape with a centimeter ruler. Find the perimeter.

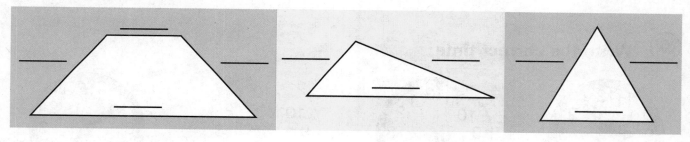

_____ _____   _____ _____   _____ _____

③ Write <, >, or =.

8 ounces = 1 cup   2 pints = 1 quart

2 cups = 1 pint   4 quarts = 1 gallon

10 ounces _____ 1 cup	4 quarts _____ 1 gallon	1 pint _____ 2 quarts
2 cups _____ 1 pint	1 quart _____ 1 pint	1 cup _____ 14 ounces

④ Find the sum.

1,062	2,271	1,301	2,453	4,736	3,004
2,951	3,685	1,783	4,465	2,190	4,941
+2,151	+1,920	+4,662	+1,850	+1,952	+1,963

5 **Put a dot (●) at the intersection. Connect the dots in order.**

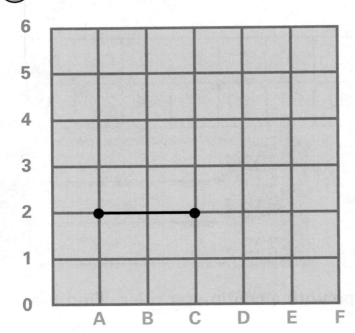

1. A 2   4. F 2   7. E 3
2. B 1   5. C 2   8. C 3
3. E 1   6. C 6

6 **Write the correct time.**

_____ : _____   _____ : _____   _____ : _____   _____ : _____

7 **Write the correct temperature and answer the questions.**

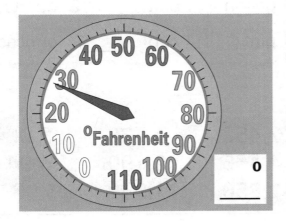

Is it hot or cold? _____

Would you wear a sweater or a

coat? _____

Would you play in the snow or

rain? _____

1 **Write the numbers.**

Is 185 closer to 100 or 200? _____

Is 160 closer to 100 or 200? _____

Is 176 closer to 100 or 200? _____

Is 138 closer to 100 or 200? _____

Is 114 closer to 100 or 200? _____

Is 127 closer to 100 or 200? _____

2 **Find the difference.**

$6.00	$4.00	$8.00	$7.00	$3.00	$9.00	$5.00
- 4.18	- 2.45	- 4.24	- 2.37	- 1.26	- 5.19	- 4.03

3 **Write the Arabic numbers.**

CLVI   = _____   DCCXCII   = _____

DCXLIII   = _____   CCCXVIII   = _____

DCCCXXV   = _____   DIX   = _____

CDXXXVII   = _____   CMLXI   = _____

4 **Mark the thermometer at the correct temperature.**
Color the liquid red.

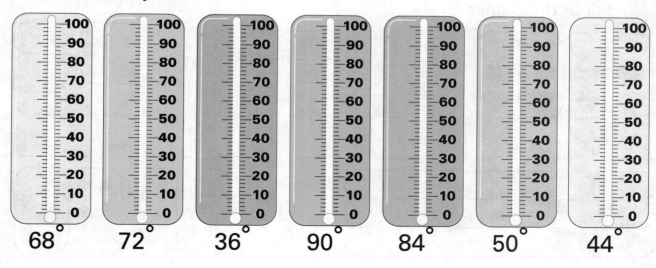

68°   72°   36°   90°   84°   50°   44°

5. Put a dot (●) at the intersection. Connect the dots in order.

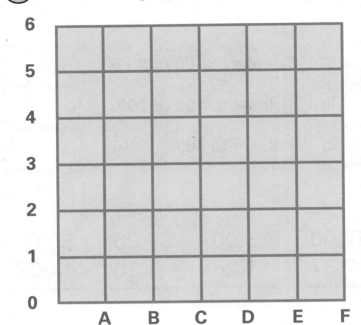

1. C 5   3. E 3   5. D 1
2. B 1   4. A 3   6. C 5

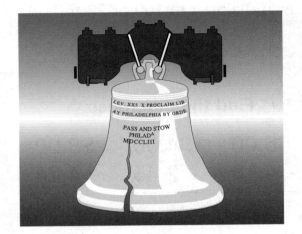

6. Find the product.

| 4
x 9 | 8
x 4 | 9
x 7 | 6
x 6 | 5
x 8 | 9
x 2 | 8
x 7 | 8
x 3 | 5
x 9 |

| 8
x 9 | 6
x 5 | 1
x 9 | 8
x 8 | 9
x 3 | 4
x 6 | 9
x 6 | 6
x 3 | 6
x 8 |

7. Fill in the blanks.

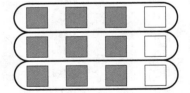

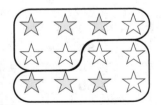

_____ of _____ = _____   _____ of _____ = _____   _____ of _____ = _____

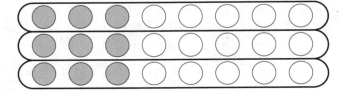

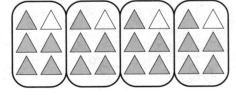

_____ of _____ = _____   _____ of _____ = _____

144

1 **Find the volume for each set by counting the cubes.**

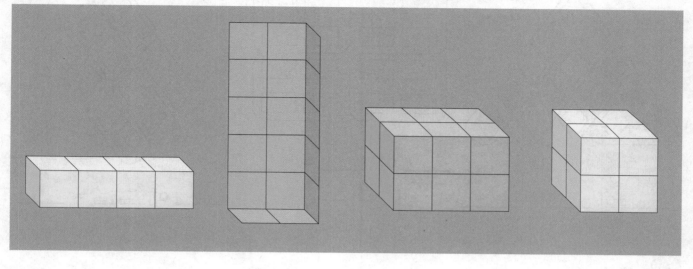

_____ cubic units _____ cubic units _____ cubic units _____ cubic units

2 **Find the difference and check.**

$4.02	$6.07	$3.01	$8.03	$2.06	$5.05	$7.04
- 2.65	- 3.78	- 1.34	- 4.26	- 1.58	- 2.49	- 3.17

3 **Write the numbers.**

Is 242 closer to 200 or 300?

Is 569 closer to 500 or 600?

Is 803 closer to 800 or 900?

Is 758 closer to 700 or 800?

Is 375 closer to 300 or 400?

Is 628 closer to 600 or 700?

Is 454 closer to 400 or 500?

Is 160 closer to 100 or 200?

4 Maria's father drove 27 miles to work. Sam's father drove 36 miles to work. Sam's father drove how many miles more than Maria's father?

⑤ Fill in the blanks.

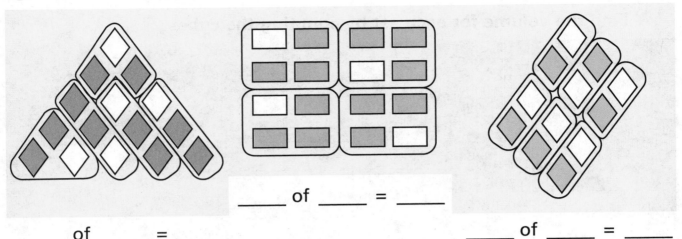

_____ of _____ = _____

_____ of _____ = _____

_____ of _____ = _____

⑥ Find the sum.

2,161	2,673	1,851	1,451	4,982	3,044
1,781	1,452	4,963	2,784	3,434	1,993
+4,921	+2,341	+2,073	+4,653	+1,173	+2,822

⑦ Find the product.

0	6	4	9	3	7	1	0	6
x 7	x 8	x 2	x 7	x 8	x 7	x 4	x 8	x 7

2	4	2	8	8	5	4	4	10
x 8	x 4	x 7	x 9	x 8	x 7	x 8	x 3	x 7

5	5	4	1	4	10	0	9	7
x 4	x 8	x 7	x 8	x 6	x 8	x 4	x 4	x 8

1 **Number the events in the order that they appear.**

_____ The teacher graded the students' math sheets.

_____ The teacher handed out the math sheets.

_____ The students completed their math sheets.

2 **Write <, >, or =.**

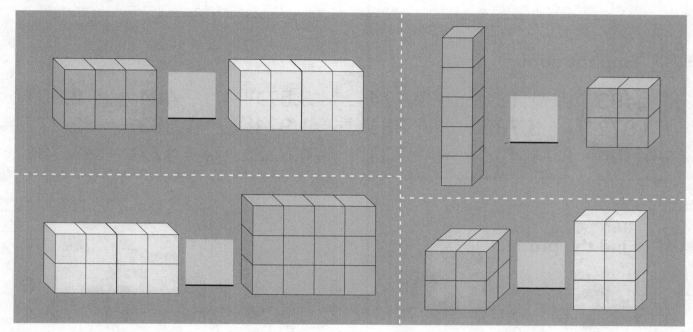

3 **Solve the equations.**

$n - 8 = 5$	$n - 4 = 9$	$n + 6 = 13$	$n + 3 = 11$

4 **Find the difference and check.**

$6.03	$2.01	$9.04	$3.06	$5.02	$7.07	$4.05
- 4.88	- 1.19	- 5.27	- 1.68	- 2.35	- 3.59	- 3.46

5 Fill in the blanks.

_____ of _____ = _____

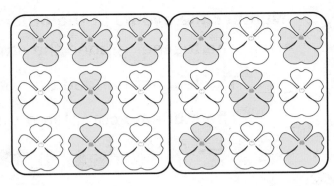

_____ of _____ = _____

6 Find the sum.

1,493	1,181	2,174	3,571	2,404	2,901
3,872	3,782	1,831	1,971	1,863	2,272
+4,304	+1,403	+3,731	+4,322	+4,472	+1,181

7 Find the product.

9	9	4	6	4	4	5	6	6
x 3	x 6	x 3	x 7	x 2	x 9	x 3	x 5	x 4

4	3	6	8	4	3	8	5	3
x 4	x 0	x 6	x 3	x 8	x 3	x 6	x 4	x 2

8 There were 86 birds on the pond. At dusk 95 more birds landed on the pond. How many birds were now on the pond?

1 **Write as a number sentence.**

Three hundred eighty plus fifty-one is four hundred

thirty-one.

_____

Two hundred fifty-three decreased by one hundred thirty-nine

is one hundred fourteen.

_____

Four hundred nine minus one hundred ten equals two hundred

ninety-nine.

_____

Five hundred twenty-seven and two hundred forty-two equals

seven hundred sixty-nine.

_____

2 **Number the events in the order that they appear.**

_____ We played baseball at recess.

_____ The teacher read us a story after recess.

_____ The bell rang for recess.

3 **Write two word problems about the pictures and solve them.**

_____   _____

_____   _____

_____   _____

_____   _____

_____   _____

_____   _____

Write <, >, or =.

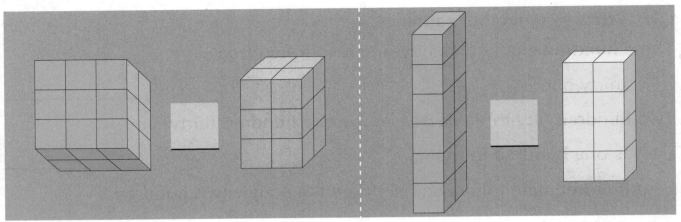

5 **Solve the equations.**

n - 5 = 6	n - 7 = 11	n + 8 = 17	n + 4 = 12

6 **Find the sum.**

1,332	4,023	3,311	4,242	2,553	2,541
1,293	2,594	1,794	3,873	4,691	1,694
+2,811	+1,871	+1,671	+1,844	+1,632	+1,532

7 **Find the product.**

7	4	6	7	4	7	2	4	6
x 9	x 7	x 5	x 8	x 1	x 1	x 7	x 4	x 3

7	4	6	7	7	4	4	9	5
x 6	x 3	x 6	x 3	x 7	x 6	x 2	x 6	x 7

1 **Shade the fractional part of each set.**

$\frac{2}{5}$ 　　　　$\frac{3}{5}$ 　　　　$\frac{5}{6}$

2 **Number the events in the order that they happen.**

_____ Mother fixes dinner.

_____ I wash the dinner dishes.

_____ The family eats dinner.

3 **Write the Roman numerals.**

458 _____   543 _____

627 _____   789 _____

962 _____   231 _____

314 _____   796 _____

4 **Write as a number sentence.**

Six hundred twenty-two increased by fifty-three is six hundred seventy-five. _____

Eight hundred seventy-one take away one hundred thirty-five is seven hundred thirty-six. _____

Five hundred eighty-four less ninety equals four hundred ninety-four. _____

151

5 Draw a line of symmetry on each shape.

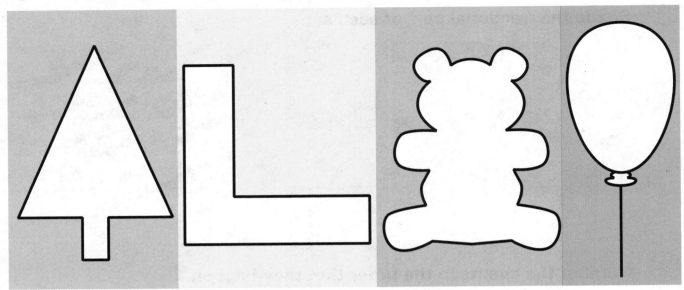

6 Write the numbers.

7 Find the difference.

901 - 515	503 - 468	206 - 139	704 - 676	402 - 223	307 - 159	605 - 347

808 - 349	501 - 162	606 - 449	403 - 217	902 - 333	305 - 159	704 - 428

1 **Circle the next picture in sequence.** **4 pts.**

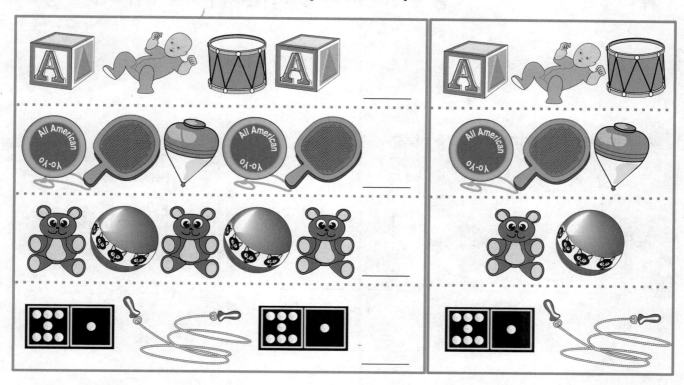

2 **Draw the lines using an inch ruler.** **3 pts.**

$3\frac{1}{4}$ inch

$5\frac{1}{2}$ inch

$2\frac{3}{4}$ inch

3 **Write as a number sentence.** **4 pts.**

Fifty increased by twenty-three equals seventy-three. _____

Thirty-one take away sixteen equals fifteen. _____

Seventy-six minus fifty-nine is seventeen. _____

Twenty-four plus forty-two is sixty-six. _____

④ **Solve the equations.** 4 pts.

n + 3 = 9	n - 8 = 5	5 + n = 11	n - 4 = 9

⑤ **Find the perimeter.** 6 pts.

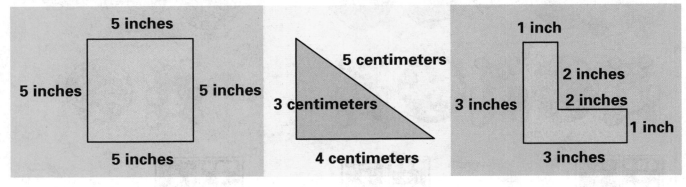

5 inches

5 inches   5 inches

5 inches

5 centimeters

3 centimeters

4 centimeters

1 inch

2 inches

2 inches

3 inches

1 inch

3 inches

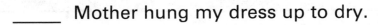

_____ _____ _____

⑥ **Number the events in the order that they happen.** 3 pts.

_____ Mother hung my dress up to dry.

_____ I ironed my dress.

_____ Mother washed my dress.

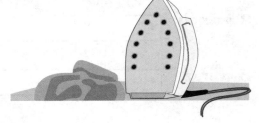

⑦ **Write a word problem about the picture.** 1 pt.

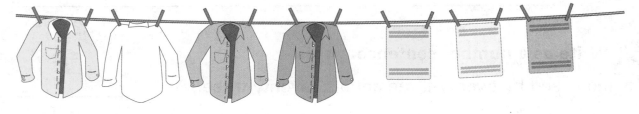

_____

_____

_____

_____

154

1 **Write the point of intersection. Connect the dots in order.**

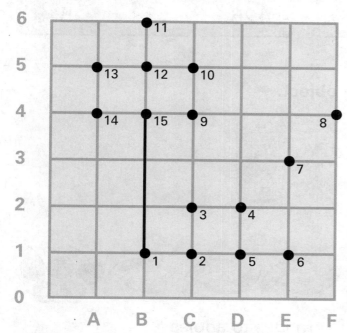

1. _____   6. _____   11. _____

2. _____   7. _____   12. _____

3. _____   8. _____   13. _____

4. _____   9. _____   14. _____

5. _____   10. _____   15. _____

2 **Write the Arabic numbers.**

CDXXXVI = _____   CMXLVII = _____

DLXXXIX = _____   CXXV = _____

DCCLIV = _____   DCCCLXIII = _____

CCCXC = _____   CCLXXVIII = _____

3 **Shade the fractional part of each set.**

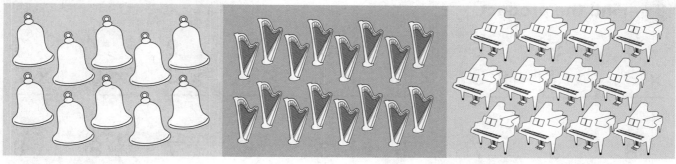

$$\frac{4}{5} \qquad\qquad \frac{3}{4} \qquad\qquad \frac{2}{3}$$

4 Find the difference.

506	803	301	902	403	704	601
- 158	- 275	- 145	- 367	- 126	- 438	- 518

5 Draw a line of symmetry on each object.

6 Write the ratio.

apples to bananas   __ : __   oranges to apples   __ : __

oranges to cherries   __ : __   cherries to apples   __ : __

bananas to oranges   __ : __   bananas to cherries   __ : __

7 Find the sum.

1,191	2,081	1,924	1,740	1,953	4,334
2,791	1,733	2,261	4,781	1,561	1,670
+4,501	+2,962	+2,382	+3,158	+4,242	+3,645

8 Find the product.

4	9	5	4	3	6	9	7	3
x 3	x 7	x 3	x 8	x 3	x 7	x 3	x 0	x 2

8	8	7	5	3	8	7	8	8
x 7	x 8	x 1	x 8	x 6	x 3	x 3	x 6	x 2

1 **Write the numbers.**

1 day	= _____	hours
1 week	= _____	days
1 year	= _____	weeks
1 pound	= _____	ounces

1 hour	= _____	minutes
1 minute	= _____	seconds
1 year	= _____	months
1 ton	= _____	pounds

2 **Write the name of each solid.**

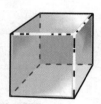    

_____ _____ _____ _____ _____

3 **Find the sum.**

1,143	1,613	6,546	1,133	3,437	1,355
2,286	3,748	1,829	1,795	2,656	3,751
+3,925	+4,092	+1,380	+3,429	+1,274	+1,849

4 **Find the difference and check.**

421	642	727	952	816	525	843
- 247	- 159	- 339	- 485	- 128	- 376	- 597

914	721	673		538	331	916
- 266	- 684	- 289		- 169	- 158	- 657

5 Write the correct time.

___ : ___   ___ : ___   ___ : ___   ___ : ___

6 Write the point of intersection. Connect the dots in order.

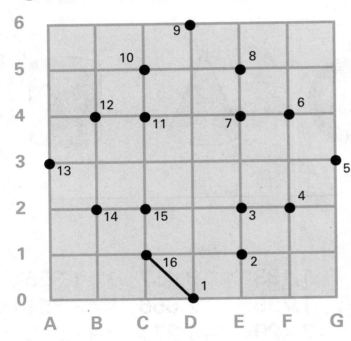

1. _____   6. _____   11. _____

2. _____   7. _____   12. _____

3. _____   8. _____   13. _____

4. _____   9. _____   14. _____

5. _____   10. _____   15. _____

                          16. _____

7 Write the ratio.

soccer balls to baseballs ___ : ___	baseballs to footballs ___ : ___
basketballs to footballs ___ : ___	basketballs to soccer balls ___ : ___

8 Find the product.

X	5	3	6	9	2	8	4	7
9								

X	7	4	8	0	6	3	5	1
4								

1 Circle the next shape in sequence.

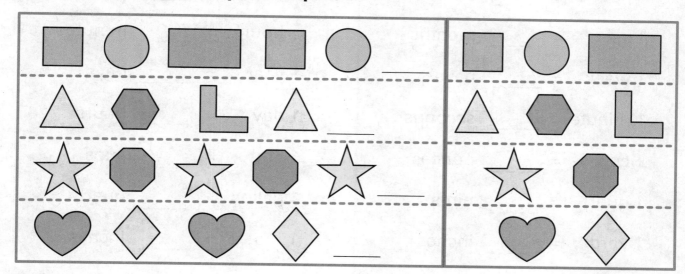

2 Draw both hands on the clock.

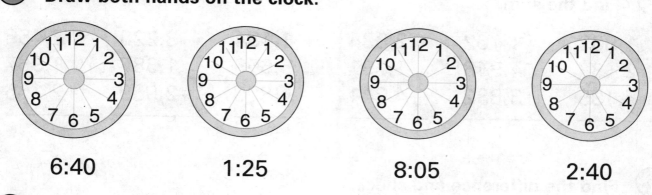

| 6:40 | 1:25 | 8:05 | 2:40 |

3 Find the product.

$\begin{array}{r} 7 \\ \times\ 7 \\ \hline \end{array}$	$\begin{array}{r} 8 \\ \times\ 4 \\ \hline \end{array}$	$\begin{array}{r} 9 \\ \times\ 2 \\ \hline \end{array}$	$\begin{array}{r} 1 \\ \times\ 7 \\ \hline \end{array}$	$\begin{array}{r} 9 \\ \times\ 8 \\ \hline \end{array}$	$\begin{array}{r} 4 \\ \times\ 2 \\ \hline \end{array}$	$\begin{array}{r} 9 \\ \times\ 3 \\ \hline \end{array}$	$\begin{array}{r} 7 \\ \times\ 3 \\ \hline \end{array}$	$\begin{array}{r} 4 \\ \times\ 6 \\ \hline \end{array}$
$\begin{array}{r} 9 \\ \times\ 4 \\ \hline \end{array}$	$\begin{array}{r} 6 \\ \times\ 7 \\ \hline \end{array}$	$\begin{array}{r} 5 \\ \times\ 9 \\ \hline \end{array}$	$\begin{array}{r} 3 \\ \times\ 4 \\ \hline \end{array}$	$\begin{array}{r} 8 \\ \times\ 3 \\ \hline \end{array}$	$\begin{array}{r} 7 \\ \times\ 5 \\ \hline \end{array}$	$\begin{array}{r} 4 \\ \times\ 7 \\ \hline \end{array}$	$\begin{array}{r} 8 \\ \times\ 8 \\ \hline \end{array}$	$\begin{array}{r} 10 \\ \times\ 4 \\ \hline \end{array}$
$\begin{array}{r} 5 \\ \times\ 8 \\ \hline \end{array}$	$\begin{array}{r} 4 \\ \times\ 4 \\ \hline \end{array}$	$\begin{array}{r} 10 \\ \times\ 7 \\ \hline \end{array}$	$\begin{array}{r} 2 \\ \times\ 7 \\ \hline \end{array}$	$\begin{array}{r} 7 \\ \times\ 8 \\ \hline \end{array}$	$\begin{array}{r} 5 \\ \times\ 4 \\ \hline \end{array}$	$\begin{array}{r} 6 \\ \times\ 8 \\ \hline \end{array}$	$\begin{array}{r} 4 \\ \times\ 0 \\ \hline \end{array}$	$\begin{array}{r} 9 \\ \times\ 9 \\ \hline \end{array}$

4 **Write the numbers.**

1 pound = _____ ounces	1 ton = _____ pounds
1 year = _____ months	$\frac{1}{2}$ hour = _____ minutes
1 week = _____ days	1 year = _____ days
1 minute = _____ seconds	1 day = _____ hours
1 cup = _____ ounces	1 pint = _____ cups
1 quart = _____ pints	1 gallon = _____ quarts
1 yard = _____ inches	1 foot = _____ inches

5 **Find the sum.**

1,803	1,162	2,834	1,184	3,220	2,456
2,487	4,948	1,797	5,669	1,387	1,967
+5,195	+3,832	+4,241	+1,806	+2,939	+2,155

6 **Find the difference and check.**

410	914	432	925	803	726	531
- 395	- 738	- 86	- 377	- 274	- 149	- 37

7 Mother planted 5 rows of tomato plants. There were 8 plants in each row. How many tomato plants did she plant?

1 **Write the correct temperature.**

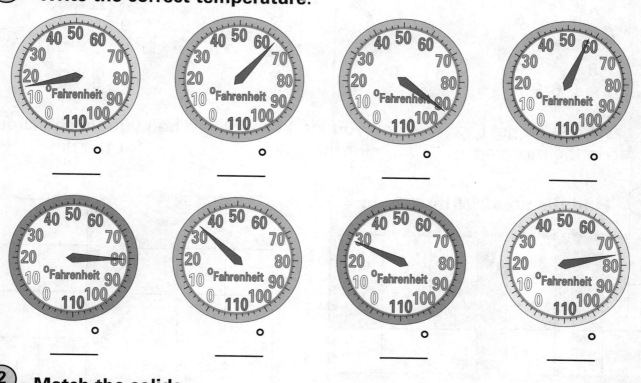

° ___   ° ___   ° ___   ° ___

° ___   ° ___   ° ___   ° ___

2 **Match the solids.**

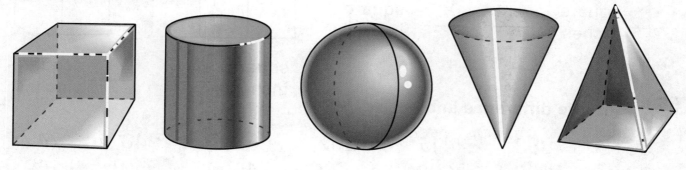

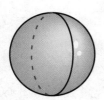  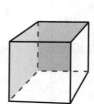  

3 The orange tree had 85 oranges on it. Jed's mother told him to pick one dozen oranges. How many oranges were left on the tree?

161

4 Draw both hands on the clocks.

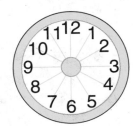
When you get
up in the morning

When you start school
for the day

When you finish school
for the day

5 Find the area. Write <, >, or =.

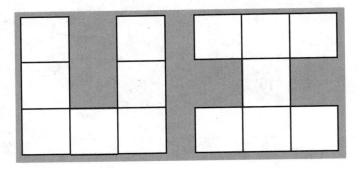

_____ square   _____ _____ square
inches   inches

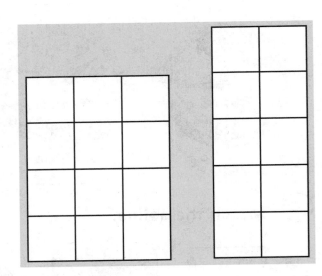

_____ square   _____ _____ square
inches   inches

6 Find the difference and check.

961	853	417	202	520	940	742
- 874	- 167	- 189	- 37	- 456	- 49	- 169

7 Find the product.

8	7	8	4	7	8	5	10	9
x 2	x 2	x 7	x 8	x 1	x 3	x 7	x 8	x 7

5	6	8	7		8	7	4	7
x 8	x 7	x 9	x 3		x 8	x 0	x 7	x 7

162

①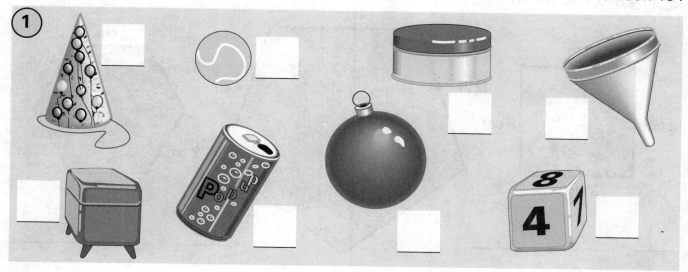

Put a **B** by each cube.   Put a **C** by each cylinder.

Put a **N** by each cone.   Put a **S** by each sphere.

② **Find the sum.**

32	26	11	21	21	12	48	13
23	24	13	16	22	13	12	39
14	23	14	17	13	24	13	21
+16	+11	+18	+24	+34	+19	+21	+15

③ **Mark the thermometer at the correct temperature.**
Draw a red pointer.

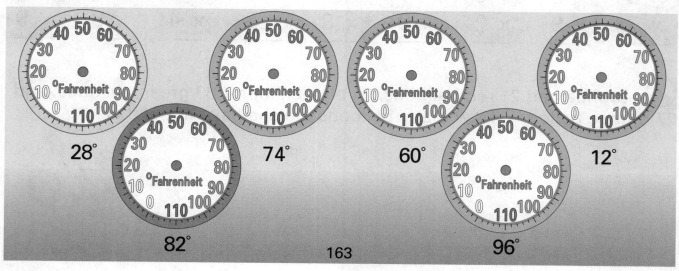

28°   74°   60°   12°

82°   96°

4 **Find the perimeter.**

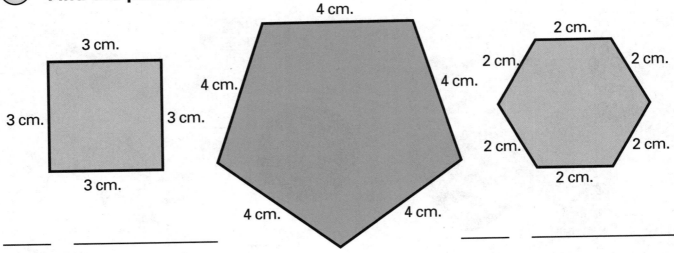

3 cm. 3 cm. 3 cm. 3 cm.

4 cm. 4 cm. 4 cm. 4 cm. 4 cm.

2 cm. 2 cm. 2 cm. 2 cm. 2 cm. 2 cm.

_____ _____

_____ _____

5 **Find the difference.**

926	751	514	603	830	327	705
- 469	- 486	- 128	- 358	- 542	- 138	- 577

6 **Find the product.**

6	8	9	1	5	10	0	8	9
x 9	x 0	x 5	x 9	x 8	x 9	x 9	x 1	x 3

8	2	8	7	4	8	9	3	9
x 7	x 9	x 2	x 9	x 8	x 9	x 4	x 8	x 9

7 Brenda had 21 red balloons, 14 blue balloons, 33 green balloons, and 27 orange balloons. How many balloons did she have altogether?

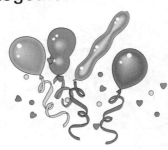

164

1 Write the correct temperature.

_____ _____ _____ _____ _____ _____

2 Draw a line graph using the temperatures above.

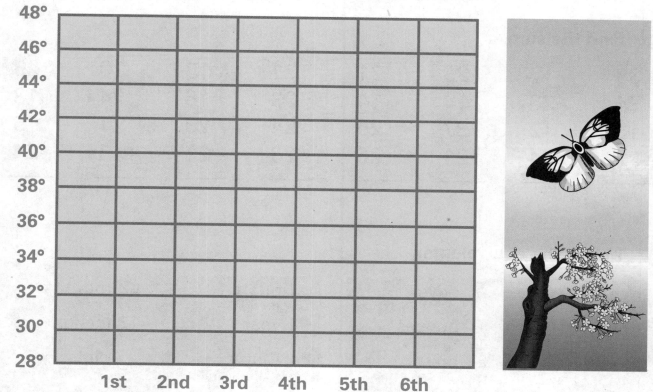

3 Find the difference.

251 - 193	514 - 399	624 - 287	403 - 245	840 - 451	712 - 374	961 - 785

④ Find the volume.

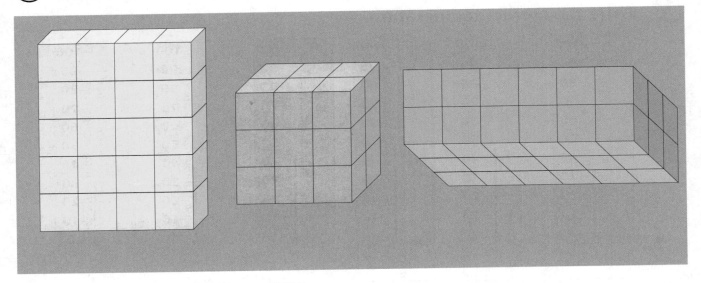

_____ cubic units   _____ cubic units   _____ cubic units

⑤ Find the sum.

38	17	23	21	21	15	29	25
24	23	14	14	23	16	24	13
13	12	37	25	24	23	21	15
+22	+34	+21	+26	+26	+21	+13	+24
___	___	___	___	___	___	___	___

⑥ Match the equivalents.

1 cup	7 days
1 pint	8 ounces
1 hour	24 hours
1 week	2 cups
1 day	60 minutes
1 year	52 weeks

1 quart	12 months
1 year	12 inches
1 foot	2 pints
1 minute	3 feet
1 gallon	4 quarts
1 yard	60 seconds

1 **Write the letter on the blank.**

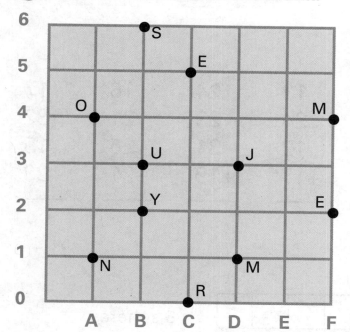

C 5 ____   B 6 ____

A 1 ____   B 3 ____

D 3 ____   D 1 ____

A 4 ____   F 4 ____

B 2 ____   F 2 ____

C 0 ____

2 **Solve the equations.**

$n + 2 = 9$	$n - 6 = 14$	$n - 9 = 15$	$8 + n = 16$

3 **Find the difference.**

1,643 - 1,179	7,380 - 2,298	8,503 - 2,226	7,613 - 6,494	8,460 - 3,389	8,628 - 6,569

4 **Find the product.**

X	5	7	9	4	6	3	2
6							

X	3	1	5	4	0	7	2
7							

X	3	7	5	8	4	6
8						

X	4	3	9	5	8	7
9						

5 Find the sum.

33	28	23	11	13	24	16	17
16	33	29	14	24	23	21	32
24	24	24	23	12	31	25	15
+22	+12	+22	+27	+17	+19	+21	+23

6 Draw a bar graph.

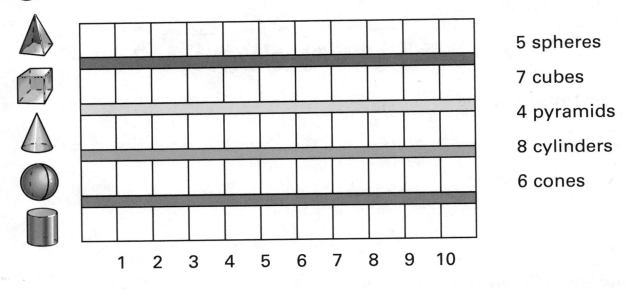

5 spheres

7 cubes

4 pyramids

8 cylinders

6 cones

1 2 3 4 5 6 7 8 9 10

7 Match the Roman numerals to the Arabic numbers.

65	CLXXXIII	47	DXCVI
183	CMXXXVIII	429	DCCLII
374	LXV	596	XLVII
938	CCCLXXIV	752	CDXXIX

168

1 Draw the pictograph.

Weight of Dogs

Tipper		each
Brix		
Patch		equals
Rags		10 pounds
Dandy		

Tipper – 30 lbs.   Brix – 50 lbs.   Patch – 10 lbs.

Rags – 70 lbs.   Dandy – 20 lbs.

2 Find the sum.

11	21	24	11	21	21	12	13
35	13	23	23	15	31	23	39
26	4	18	14	26	15	14	21
+22	+39	+22	+17	+13	+26	+27	+15

3 Find the difference.

9,830	6,712	6,915	7,930	7,624	6,915
- 3,785	- 2,054	- 3,237	- 2,567	- 4,085	- 4,679

4 Number the events in the order that they happen.

_____ Winter vacation

_____ School is out

_____ Spring break

__1__ Thanksgiving

169

5 Write the point of intersection. Connect the dots in order.

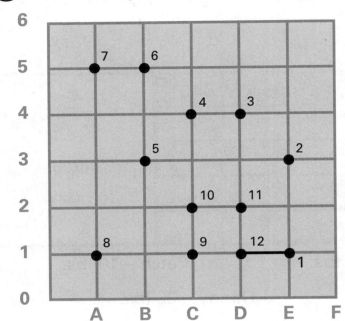

1. _____
2. _____
3. _____
4. _____
5. _____
6. _____
7. _____
8. _____
9. _____
10. _____
11. _____
12. _____

6 Write the Arabic numbers.

CCCLXXII   =   _____   CDLXXXV   =   _____

DLXIV   =   _____   CMXVIII   =   _____

7 Write the numbers.

1 pint	= _____	cups
1 hour	= _____	minutes
1 year	= _____	days
1 yard	= _____	feet
1 day	= _____	hours

1 gallon	= _____	quarts
1 week	= _____	days
1 foot	= _____	inches
1 pound	= _____	ounces
1 year	= _____	months

8 Find the product.

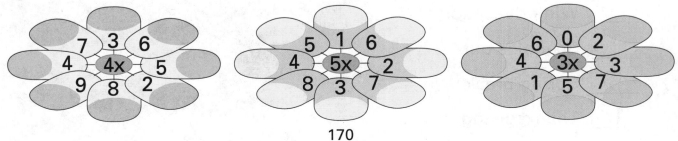

170

1 **Write the numbers.**

4 + 4 = _____	6 + 6 = _____	2 + 2 = _____
$\frac{1}{2}$ of 8 = _____	$\frac{1}{2}$ of 12 = _____	$\frac{1}{2}$ of 4 = _____
5 + 5 = _____	7 + 7 = _____	8 + 8 = _____
$\frac{1}{2}$ of 10 = _____	$\frac{1}{2}$ of 14 = _____	$\frac{1}{2}$ of 16 = _____
3 + 3 = _____	1 + 1 = _____	9 + 9 = _____
$\frac{1}{2}$ of 6 = _____	$\frac{1}{2}$ of 2 = _____	$\frac{1}{2}$ of 18 = _____

2 **Write the numbers.**

4 x _____ = 24	9 x _____ = 54	7 x _____ = 63	9 x _____ = 36
8 x _____ = 72	4 x _____ = 28	6 x _____ = 24	3 x _____ = 18
2 x _____ = 14	5 x _____ = 45	3 x _____ = 6	5 x _____ = 20
6 x _____ = 18	8 x _____ = 16	7 x _____ = 35	2 x _____ = 10
4 x _____ = 36	6 x _____ = 48	3 x _____ = 24	2 x _____ = 18
2 x _____ = 8	5 x _____ = 35	7 x _____ = 28	8 x _____ = 24
3 x _____ = 9	7 x _____ = 42	6 x _____ = 12	9 x _____ = 45

3 **Find the sum.**

41	12	63	51	42	11	42	42
32	41	53	14	81	73	32	62
23	51	11	11	13	42	21	13
+72	+61	+31	+62	+31	+32	+92	+72
_____	_____	_____	_____	_____	_____	_____	_____

171

(4) **Number the events in the order that they happen.**

_____ Wednesday's baseball game

_____ Tuesday's piano lesson

__1__ Monday's doctor's appointment

_____ Saturday's birthday party

(5) **Write the correct words.**

12 inches = 1 _____

4 quarts = 1 _____

60 minutes = 1 _____

7 days = 1 _____

2,000 pounds = 1 _____

12 months = 1 _____

2 pints = 1 _____

3 feet = 1 _____

24 hours = 1 _____

16 ounces = 1 _____

(6) **Find the difference and check.**

2,912	7,803	5,641	5,957	4,820	7,364
- 2,645	- 5,617	- 1,568	- 4,368	- 2,394	- 1,078

(7) Josh had 36 Cubs baseball cards. He gave 8 of them to Joseph. How many Cubs baseball cards does Josh have left?

Cindy had 7 girls at her birthday party. She gave each of them 3 suckers. How many suckers did Cindy give to the girls?

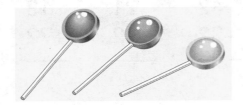

172

1 **Look at the map and write the answers.**

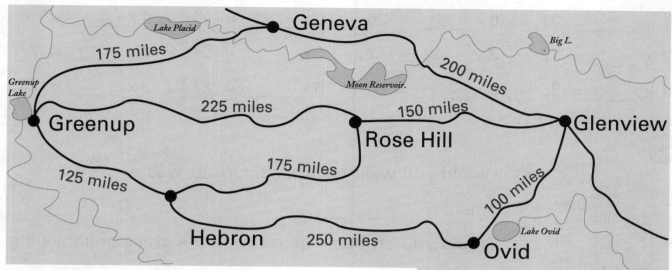

How far is it from:

Greenup to Hebron _____

Rose Hill to Glenview _____

Hebron to Rose Hill _____

Geneva to Glenview to Ovid _____

Hebron to Ovid _____

What is the shortest way to get from Greenup to Glenview?

_____

_____

2 **Write the numbers.**

2 + 2 = _____	5 + 5 = _____	9 + 9 = _____
$\frac{1}{2}$ of 4 = _____	$\frac{1}{2}$ of 10 = _____	$\frac{1}{2}$ of 18 = _____
6 + 6 = _____	8 + 8 = _____	7 + 7 = _____
$\frac{1}{2}$ of 12 = _____	$\frac{1}{2}$ of 16 = _____	$\frac{1}{2}$ of 14 = _____

3 **Write the numbers.**

4 x _____ = 20   8 x _____ = 40   4 x _____ = 8   9 x _____ = 18

7 x _____ = 21   6 x _____ = 36   5 x _____ = 40   4 x _____ = 16

2 x _____ = 12   3 x _____ = 12   6 x _____ = 54   3 x _____ = 27

8 x _____ = 56   6 x _____ = 30   9 x _____ = 27   3 x _____ = 21

4

Would you wear a shirt, coat, or a sweater

outside? _____

Would you probably be mowing the grass or shoveling

snow? _____

Would you want to eat ice cream or drink hot

chocolate after being outside? _____

5 **Find the sum.**

52	66	54	65	84	67	29	32
11	11	32	16	31	31	34	41
63	54	63	11	49	14	43	13
+44	+27	+16	+54	+13	+43	+82	+22

6   Shari colored 6 pictures on Monday, 4 pictures on Tuesday, 3 pictures on Wednesday, and 5 pictures on Thursday. How many pictures did she color in the four days?

174

1 **Write the numbers.**

$\frac{1}{2}$ of 10 = _____	$\frac{1}{2}$ of 16 = _____	$\frac{1}{2}$ of 8 = _____
$\frac{1}{2}$ of 18 = _____	$\frac{1}{2}$ of 6 = _____	$\frac{1}{2}$ of 12 = _____
$\frac{1}{2}$ of 2 = _____	$\frac{1}{2}$ of 14 = _____	$\frac{1}{2}$ of 4 = _____

2 **Write the correct words.**

16 ounces   = 1 _____   52 weeks   = 1 _____

365 days   = 1 _____   2 cups   = 1 _____

60 seconds = 1 _____   30 minutes = $\frac{1}{2}$ _____

36 inches   = 1 _____   12 inches   = 1 _____

3 **Mark the thermometer at the correct temperature.**
Color the liquid red.

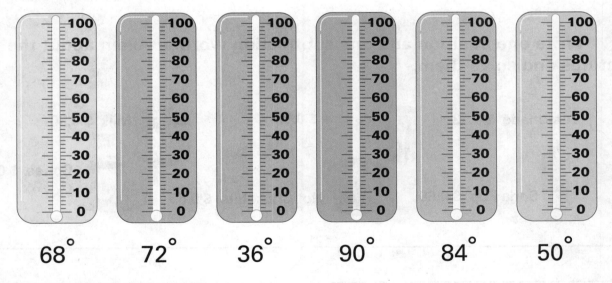

68°   72°   36°   90°   84°   50°

4 **Find the difference.**

8,947 - 1,269	8,226 - 3,159	8,451 - 5,179	9,802 - 1,489	3,631 - 2,067	9,620 - 9,479

5 **Look at the map and write the answers.**

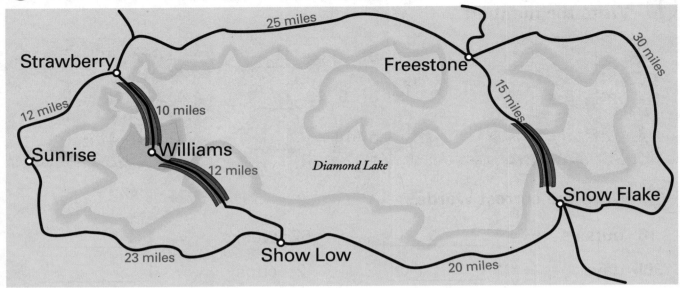

How much closer is Snow Flake to Freestone if you go over the bridge rather than around the lake? _____

Williams is how much closer to Strawberry than Show Low? _____

What is the closest town to Sunrise? _____

6 **Write one addition and one subtraction word problem about the pictures and solve them.**

Lemonade $ 0.73   Ice Tea $ 0.59   Milk $ 0.50

Soda Pop $ 0.60   Hot Chocolate $ 0.55   Coffee $ 0.55

_____   _____

_____   _____

_____   _____

_____   _____

_____   _____

_____   _____

176

1 **Write the temperature.**   6 pts.

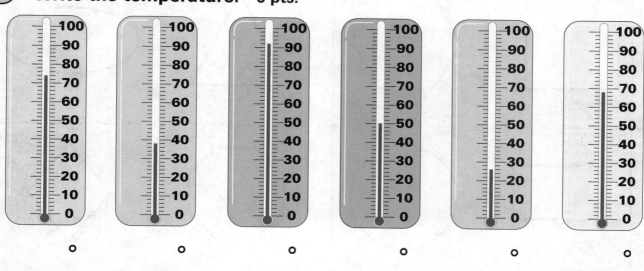

_____   _____   _____   _____   _____   _____

2 **Write the ratio.**   6 pts.

birds to fish   ___ : ___   butterflies to lambs   ___ : ___

lambs to fish   ___ : ___   birds to butterflies   ___ : ___

butterflies and birds to fish and lambs   ___ : ___

fish and butterflies to lambs and birds   ___ : ___

3 **Write the correct time.**   4 pts.

:   :   :   :

_____   _____   _____   _____

4 **Name the shape. Draw a line of symmetry for each shape. 8 pts.**

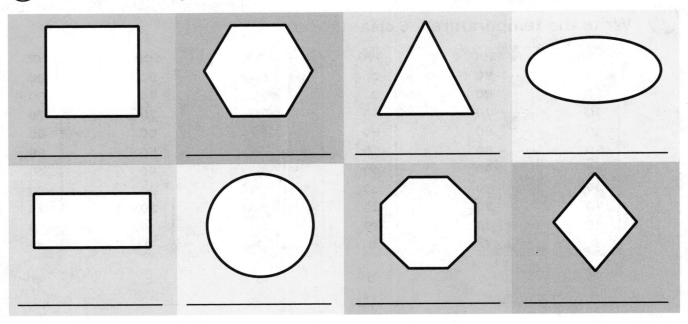

5 **Write the Arabic numbers.   6 pts.**

CCCXCV   = _____   XXXVI   = _____

LXXIV   = _____   CXXVII   = _____

DCCCLXIX   = _____   DCXLII   = _____

6 **Circle the next picture in sequence.   4 pts.**

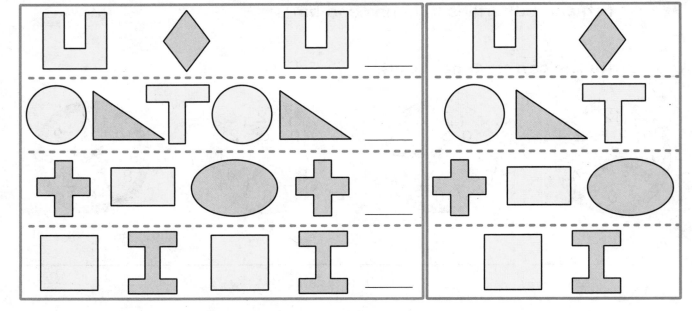

178

(7) Find the area. 3 pts.

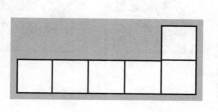

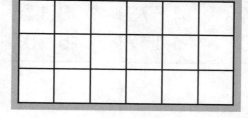

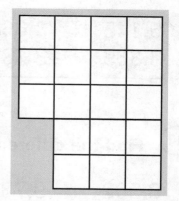

_____ square units

_____ square units

_____ square units

(8) Find the volume. 3 pts.

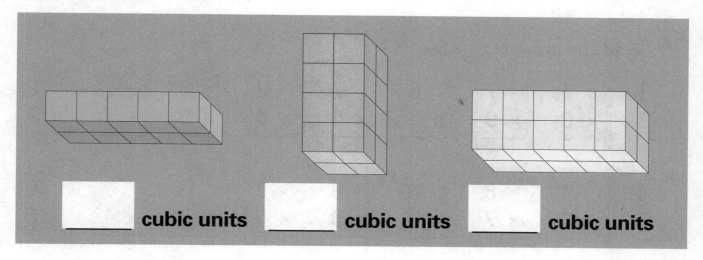

_____ **cubic units**   _____ **cubic units**   _____ **cubic units**

(9) Fill in the blanks. 6 pts.

_____ of _____ = _____

_____ of _____ = _____

179

10 **Find the sum.** 6 pts.

5,145	3,664	4,573	3,176	4,228	2,689
+3,369	+3,188	+5,157	+5,785	+4,485	+6,284

11 **Find the difference.** 6 pts.

8,902	9,731	6,924	7,830	9,556	8,413
- 7,837	- 4,652	- 1,539	- 3,596	- 7,389	- 2,367

12 **Find the product.** 18 pts.

3	7	7	6	7	3	9	7	2
x 3	x 0	x 9	x 6	x 4	x 4	x 9	x 7	x 7

4	3	6	8	3	7	3	7	6
x 4	x 7	x 7	x 8	x 9	x 5	x 8	x 1	x 3

13 There were 36 puppies and 28 kittens in the pet store.
There were how many more puppies than kittens?

3 pts.

There were 24 cows and 37 sheep in the barnyard.
How many animals were in the barnyard altogether?

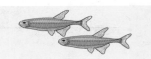

There were four fish tanks in the pet store. Each fish tank had 9 fish.
How many fish were in the four fish tanks?